lon

COSTA RICA

Robert Isenberg, Elizabeth Lavis,
Mara Vorhees, Janna Zinzi

Meet our writers

Robert Isenberg

Robert Isenberg is a writer and multimedia producer who lives in Rhode Island with his family. Find more of his work at robertisenberg.net.

Elizabeth Lavis

Elizabeth Lavis has lived and worked all over Costa Rica, Thailand, and Georgia and traveled extensively in Southeast Asia, South America and Europe. You can find her trekking through the Andes mountains or chilling out on Costa Rica's Pacific coast. Read her work in *American Way* magazine, Huffington Post, Canadian Traveller and Lonely Planet.

Mara Vorhees

🐦 mara_vorhees

Mara is always amazed at how tiny Costa Rica packs in so much adventure, wildlife and *pura vida*. On this visit, her favorite experience was taking a night hike with her 12-year-old twins and spotting the endangered Baird's tapir (p146). Follow their adventures at havetwinswilltravel.com.

Janna Zinzi

📷 wanderwomxntravels

Janna A. Zinzi (jaz) is a travel and culture writer, and co-founder of WanderWomxn, which centers the travel adventures of women and femmes of color.

CARAGUA

*Refugio de
Vida Silvestre
rto Maquenque*

*Refugio Nacional de
Vida Silvestre
Barra del Colorado*

*Caribbean
Sea*

○ Tortuguero

Puerto Viejo
de Sarapiquí

○ La Virgen

*Parque
Nacional
Tortuguero*

○ San Miguel

○ Parismina

△ *Volcán Poás*

○ Guácimo

an José &
ntral Valley 42

Siquirres

*Parque
Nacional
Braulio
Carrillo*

*Parque
Nacional
Barbilla*

Caribbean Coast 82

eredia ●

● Limón City

△ SAN JOSÉ

○ Turrialba

de

*Limón
City
1 hr* ✈

*Parque Nacional
Tapantí-Macizo
Cerro la Muerte*

Cahuita ○

Puerto Viejo

acific
82

● San Gerardo
de Dota

○ Quepos

*Río
Savegre*

*Parque
Nacional
Chirripó*

Bribrí○

○ ● Manzanillo

Río Telira

○ ● Sixaola

ntonio○

○ San Gerardo de Rivas

○ Rivas

*rque Nacional
anuel Antonio*

● San Isidro
de El General

*Parque
Internacional
La Amistad*

○ Dominical

Río General

○ Uvita

○ Buenos Aires

Southern Costa Rica &
Península de Osa 208

*Bahía de
Coronado*

○ Sierpe

*Bahía
Drake* Agujitas

*Parque Nacional
Piedras Blancas*

Río Claro ○

Isla del Caño ○

*Parque
Nacional
Corcovado*

*Golfo
Dulce*

PANAMA

○ Paso Canoas

*Península
de Osa*

Puerto
Jiménez

*San José
1 hr* ✈

○ Carate

Pavones

*Golfo de
Chiriquí*

**Experience
Costa Rica
online**

■■■■ Ride the waves and relax in the sand. Make sense of the present by learning about the past. Pump that adrenaline with natural adventure activities. Energize your taste buds with coffee and chocolate. Be amazed by awesome volcanoes. Soak up culture and history in the bustling capital. Retreat to the country. Immerse yourself in wildlife and wilder landscapes. Refresh your body and mind at gushing cascades.

This is Costa Rica.

TURN THE PAGE AND START PLANNING YOUR NEXT BEST TRIP →

Peñas Blancas

Lago de
Nicaragua

Islas
Solentiname

N I

La Cruz

Santa Cecilia

Los Chiles

*Golfo de
Santa Elena*

*Parque
Nacional
Guanacaste*

Upala

*Refugio de
Vida Silvestre
Caño Negro*

*Islas
Murciélago*

*Parque
Nacional
Santa Rosa*

*Parque
Nacional
Rincón
de la Vieja*

**Northern
Costa Rica 112**

Mi.

*Golfo de
Papagayo*

Liberia ●

*Sámara
1 hr*

*Parque Nacional
Volcán Tenorio*

*Volcán
Arenal*

Bagaces ○

*Laguna de
Arenal*

El Castillo ○

○ **La Fortuna**

San José
2½ hrs

**Ciudad
Quesad**

Potrero ○

*Parque
Nacional
Palo Verde*

Cañas ○

Santa Elena ○

*Parque
Nacional
Volcán
Arenal*

Tamarindo ○

Puerto Humo ○

Monteverde

Paraíso ○

Nicoya ○

*Isla
Chira*

○ Manzanillo

San Ramón ●

Zarcero ○

S
Ce

Península de Nicoya 156

Puntarenas

Barranca

H

Ciudad Colón

○ Sámara

*Península
de Nicoya*

Paquera ○

*Golfo de
Nicoya*

Santiago
Purisca

Santa Teresa ○
Mal País ○

○ Montezuma

San José
1½ hrs

Jacó ●

**Central P
Coast**

*Reserva Natural
Cabo Blanco*

Parrita ○

Manuel Ar
P
M

*PACIFIC
OCEAN*

N

0 ───────────────── 100 km
0 ───────────────── 50 miles

Red-eyed tree frog (p125)

Contents

Volcán Poás (p55)

SAND &
SURF

Costa Rica's beaches are world renowned for their relaxing sands and crashing waves. Surfers come from all over the world to compete here or to hone their skills, while adventurous novices visit to take lessons from the best. For travelers seeking a more low-key experience, many beaches are perfect for wading or leisurely lounging.

→ SURFING THE EQUATOR

Situated near the equator, Costa Rica's geographical position makes it the perfect surfing destination. The Pacific coast receives swells from both hemispheres all year round.

Left Sámara (p170) **Right** Surfer Merary Jimenez **Below** Tortuga Island (p167)

LEARN TO SURF

Surf camps are plentiful on Península de Nicoya and are an immersive way to learn to surf. Beginners and pros can level up their skills in seven to 10 days.

▶ Learn to ride the waves (p169)

↑ BABY TURTLES BONANZA

The Península de Nicoya is one of the few places you can see an *arribada*, a mass turtle hatching. Thousands of sea turtles are born and swim out to sea.

▶ Witness an *arribada* (p160) and learn how you can help protect sea turtles (p176)

Best Beach Experiences

▶ Ride the Caribbean waves like a local at Playa Cocles in Puerto Viejo. (p87)

▶ Sunbathe under Sámara's swaying palm trees. (p170)

▶ Cheer for the country's best at a sunset surf competition on Playa Hermosa. (p201)

▶ Visit Costa Rica's most popular surf destination, Tamarindo. (p171)

TAKE A TRIP
BACK IN TIME

One way to truly get acquainted with Costa Rica is through its history. The legacy and present-day contributions of its indigenous communities are ever-present throughout the country.

There are a multitude of ways to learn about how Spanish colonialism in the 1500s and Jamaican immigration in the 1800s shaped Costa Rica's cultural past and present.

→ ANCIENT ARCHEOLOGY

Diquís spheres are perfectly symmetrical yet mysterious stones created by Costa Rica's pre-Columbian societies. They have become a symbol of indigenous culture and history.

▶ Learn about Costa Rica's pre-Columbian history at El Sitio Museo Finca 6 (p219)

Left Museo Nacional (p63), San José **Right** Diquís spheres **Below** Blue morpho butterfly

WHO WAS JUAN SANTAMARÍA?

The name Juan Santamaría, the country's most celebrated war hero, is ever-present around Costa Rica. The drummer boy carried the torch that burned down enemy US mercenaries.

▶ Get to know Costa Rica's war hero Juan Santamaría (p51)

↑ MORPHOS METAMORPHOSIS

A highlight of the Museo Nacional is the butterfly garden. Observe 14 different species of butterflies, including the blue morpho, and learn about the plants that give them sanctuary.

▶ Wander the butterfly garden of San José's Museo Nacional (p63)

Best History Experiences

▶ **Engage with Costa Rica's past through archeological artifacts and pre-Columbian art at Museo Nacional.** (p63)

▶ **View mystical pre-Columbian stone spheres at the Finca 6 Unesco World Heritage Site.** (p219)

▶ **Connect with the Boruca tribe's powerful history and culture at Museo Boruca.** (p235)

EXTREME
EXCURSIONS

▬▬▬ The country's diverse and majestic terrain makes it the perfect place for outdoor adventures. Extreme-sports enthusiasts can take to the water for death-defying activities like whitewater rafting or swimming with sharks at world-class diving sites, to the land for rock climbing and mountain biking, or to the air for flying above the forest on ziplines.

→ EXTREME BIKING

Mountains aren't just for hiking; bikers are welcome too. The Central Valley has numerous trails and adventure parks catering both to beginners and more experienced riders.

▶ Explore the many mountain bike trails (p55)

Left Zipline, Santa Elena (p153)
Right Mountain biking, Heredia (p55)
Below Whale shark

ROCK STEADY

Rock climbing is a popular way to experience Costa Rica's stunning natural environment. An exhilarating hike to La Leona Waterfall includes cliff jumping and cavern crawling.

▶ Hike, climb, crawl and jump your way to La Leona Waterfall (p143)

↑ SWIM WITH SHARKS

Isla del Caño is a scuba-diver's dream. Visitors come for the crystal-clear visibility and extreme biodiversity, including whale sharks, sea turtles and octopuses.

▶ Dive into the crystal waters of Isla del Caño (p218)

Best Extreme Experiences

▶ **Summit Cerro Chirripó, Costa Rica's highest peak.** (p214)

▶ **Soar through the cloud forest in Santa Elena on the longest zipline in Latin America.** (p153)

▶ **Ride the rapids of the Río Savegre near Quepos.** (p191)

↘ COFFEE FACTS

1,365,000 60kg bags of coffee are produced annually.

Costa Rica produces 1% of the world's coffee.

Cacao beans were used as currency as recently as the 1930s.

CAFFEINE FIX

▬▬▬ Costa Rica offers some of the tastiest coffee and chocolate on the planet. While the highlands are ideal for growing artisanal coffee, the humid tropical climate of the Talamanca Mountains is perfect for growing the cacao fruit plant. Indigenous communities have long respected cacao and many tours will show you the process of transforming the sweet juicy fruit into a savory drink or dessert.

Best Cacao Experiences

▶ Discover how little red berries become coffee at Mi Cafecito coffee cooperative in San Miguel de Sarapiquí. (p137)

▶ Sip some of Costa Rica's best coffee at CoopeDota, a coffee cooperative based in Santa María. (p213)

▶ Learn about indigenous traditions and the cacao plant in Térraba. (p216)

↘ HOT SPOTS

Volcán Rincón de la Vieja
Costa Rica's most recent major eruption (2022)

National geo-thermal capacity
13% to 15% of the power grid

Number of active volcanoes
Five

Best Volcano Experiences

▶ Hike up hardened lava flow for epic views of Volcán Arenal. (p118)

▶ Visit Volcán Irazú, Costa Rica's highest volcano. (p68)

▶ Submerge your body in natural thermal pools and flowing turquoise rivers at Volcán Rincon de la Vieja. (p140)

▶ Witness a steaming volcanic lake at Volcán Poás. (pictured above; p55)

VOLCANO
VOLCANO VACATION

▬▬▬ A trip to Costa Rica is not complete without exploring one of the country's world-renowned volcanoes. Clustered near San José in the northwest region and Central Valley, you can visit many in one trip. You'll be treated to endless hiking trails through pristine forests, crisp mountain air and breathtaking views.

↘ CITY FACTS

San José rainfall
It rains 170 days
of the year

**Metro area
population**
1.8 million

La Sabana Park
Once was an
international
airport

CITY
SLICKERS

▬▬▬ Most tourists are drawn to Costa Rica's beaches
and mountains, but San José has a lot to offer travelers
looking to have an urban adventure. Culture and
history buffs will love learning about the country's
history preserved in the city's museums. The Museo del
Jade and Museo Nacional are a fascinating orientation
into Costa Rica's indigenous roots.

Best City Slickers Experiences

▶ Learn about Costa
Rica's most beloved
war hero at Museo
Histórico Cultural
de Juan Santamaría.
(p51)

▶ Browse the historic Mercado Central
for artisan crafts and
souvenirs. (p53)

▶ Meander around
local artists' exhibits
and outdoor sculptures at Museo de
Arte Costarricense.
(p63)

RURAL &
RUSTIC

Get to know Tico life and culture outside the tourist towns. In the remote regions of Costa Rica you'll find farms, forests and a sense of community. Experience indigenous culture through weaving and mask-making workshops. Try gold panning in rural rivers, and learn about native plants and tropical fruits from experts of the land.

Best Rural & Rustic Experiences

▶ **Learn indigenous Bribrí farming techniques outside Cahuita.** (p100)

▶ **Watch Boruca weaving and mask-making traditions.** (p217)

▶ **Visit a self-sustaining off-the-grid ranch near Arenal.** (p137)

LEFT: LINDSAY FENDT/ALAMY STOCK PHOTO ©, BOTTOM: RANCHO LA MERCED ©

→ YEEHAW!

Be a cowboy for a day at Rancho La Merced (pictured right), a working cattle ranch. Try your hand at herding cattle and calves.

▶ Try your hand on a ranch (p189)

STRIKE IT LUCKY

Try your luck at traditional gold-panning techniques in Rancho Quemado and learn about the fascinating gold-rush history of Dos Brazos.

▶ Learn about gold (p223)

Opposite Mercado Central, San José **Above** Festival de los Diablitos ceremony, Boruca (p20) **Left** Rancho La Merced

Golfo
de Santa Elena

Parque
Nacional
Santa Rosa

Golfo de
Papagayo

Potrero

Tamarindo

Paraíso

PACIFIC
OCEAN

Parque Nacional
Rincón de la Vieja

●Liberia

Upala

Bagaces

Parque
Nacional
Volcán Tenorio

Laguna
de Arenal

Cañas

Parque
Nacional
Paló Verde

Cordillera de Tilarán

Volcán
Arenal

Parque
Nacional
Volcán Arenal

Nicoya

Península
de Nicoya

Golfo de
Nicoya

Rancho
Grande

Puntarenas

Zarcero

San Ramón●

Volcán
Poás

Alajuela●

Heredia

Ciudad Colón

Santiago de
Puriscal

Tárcoles

Jacó

Parrita

Quepos
Manuel Antonio

Parque Nacional Rincon de la Vieja
Rainforest, tundra and mud pits
Experience dry and tropical rainforests, tundra and bubbling volcanic pits from three volcanoes.
🚗 *1hr from Liberia International Airport*
▶ p141

Parque Nacional Manuel Antonio
Sloths sleeping in trees
Hike the numerous trails of the country's smallest national park looking for resident wildlife. Reward yourself with playtime on the sprawling and tranquil beach.
🚗 *3hr drive from San José*
▶ p197

Parque Nacional Marino Ballena
Whale-watching hub
Spend the day on the 'Whale's Tail' beach and coastline (named for its shape). The best time to see humpback whales is between July and November.
🚗 *20min south of Dominical*
▶ p199

WILDIN'
OUT

▬▬ More than a quarter of Costa Rica's land is protected, creating a vast network of national parks. These spaces allow visitors to hike through rainforests, along highland mountain trails, and via volcanic pits and waterfalls. Part of the fun is seeing Costa Rican fauna – such as the rare tapir, famous blue morpho butterflies, raucous howler monkeys and colorful toucans – in their natural habitat.

PACIFIC
OCEAN

NICARAGUA

Caribbean
Sea

Refugio Nacional
de Vida Silvestre
Barra del Colorado

Puerto Viejo
de Sarapiquí

Tortuguero

Río Tortuguero

Parque
Nacional
Tortuguero

anta Clara

Guácimo

Siquirres

Parque
Nacional
Braulio
Carrillo

Cordillera Central

Parque
Nacional
Barbilla

Limón City

SAN JOSÉ

Cartago

Parque Nacional
Tapantí-Macizo
Cerro la Muerte

Cahuita

Puerto Viejo

Bribrí

Manzanillo

Parque
Nacional
Chirripó

Cordillera de Talamanca

Sixaola

arque Nacional
Manuel Antonio

San Isidro
de El General

Dominical

Río General

Uvita

Buenos Aires

Parque Nacional
Marino Ballena

Bahía de
Coronado

Guácimo

Sierpe

PANAMA

Bahía
Drake

Rincón

Golfo
Dulce

Parque
Nacional
Corcovado

Península
de Osa

Puerto
Jiménez

Parque Nacional Tortuguero
Crocodiles, turtles and manatees

The park consists of 172,000 hectares of protected land, canals and lagoons and is best explored by boat. Take an early morning tour to see, among others, leatherback turtles, herons, toucans, sloths, caimans, and 'Jesus Christ' lizards who skip across the water.

🚗 *1hr from San José*

▶ p90

Parque Nacional Corcovado
Tapirs in the wild

Expansive trails offer plentiful opportunities to scope out a rare tapir, watch scurrying coatis, observe monkeys swinging above your head and spy sleeping sloths.

⛴ *1hr from Bahía Drake*

▶ p224

Peninsula de Nicoya

○Paquera

Isla Tortuga

Santiago de○ Puriscal

Tárcoles○

Parque Nacional Carara

Golfo de Nicoya

Cóbano ○
Montezuma ○
Santa Teresa ○
Mal País ○

● Jacó

Reserva Natural Cabo Blanco

Río Pirrís

○ Parrita

Las Cataratas de Montezuma
Three cascading waterfalls

These three waterfalls sit along the Río Montezuma, reaching 40m high in total. Visitors can swim under all three of these falls, which flow into each other and are connected by stairs.

🚗 *40min drive from Tambor*

▶ p167

PACIFIC OCEAN

CHASING
WATERFALLS

▬▬▬ These magical natural wonders are some of the country's biggest attractions. You can find them in every corner of Costa Rica. Some are secret and secluded, and others are Insta-famous. Some are swimmable and serene, while others are rushing and gushing. Build time into your itinerary to chase waterfalls.

La Catarata Divina de Providencia
Waterfall swimming

The 3km hike to the falls through crisp cloud forest is enchanting with its changes in elevation and climate. Take a dip after the journey.

🚗 *2hr drive from San José*

▶ p213

Parque Nacional Tapantí-Macizo Cerro la Muerte

San Gerardo de Dota

Parque Nacional Los Quetzales

Quepos

Manuel Antonio

Parque Nacional Manuel Antonio

Savegre

Río Savegre

Matapalo

San Isidro de El General

Río General

Platanillo

Dominical

Cataratas Nauyaca
Refresh in canyon pools

The Río Barú creates two invigorating falls and multiple swimming holes for a family-friendly day excursion. You can access the falls via either an hour's hike or a horseback ride tour to the falls.

🚗 *20min from Dominical*

▶ p32

Parque Nacional Marino Ballena

Uvita

Peñuela

Tortuga Abajo

Bahía de Coronado

Palmar Norte

Sierpe

Río Sierpe

Chacarita

Río Chocuaco

Naguala Falls
Serene rainforest waterfalls

Three separate waterfalls are hidden within the rainforest. Hike through creeks, streams and rivers to arrive at each of these unique falls.

🚗 *30min from Bahía Drake*

▶ p221

Isla del Caño

Bahía Drake

Drake

Agujitas

Rincón

Rancho Quemado

La Palma

Parque Nacional Piedras Blancas

Parque Nacional Corcovado

Golfo Dulce

Puerto Jiménez

Laguna Corcovado

Península de Osa

N 0 / 0

50 km

25 miles

Peak Travel Season

Peak travel season begins. Demand for accommodations peaks from December through March. View tours and overnight adventures in advance at lonelyplanet.com.

← Festival de los Diablitos

From December 30 to January 2, men in the Boruca community wear masks they made and play games commemorating indigenous resistance against colonization.

● Boruca, p216

Festival de la Luz

On the second Saturday of December, Costa Rica's best bands join a massive parade of ornately lit floats followed by fireworks.

● San José

← Tope Nacional

The Tope Nacional, National Horse Parade, occurs in San José on December 26, bringing expert riders and show horses from around the country.

● San José

DECEMBER

Average daytime max: 27°C, 82°F (Pacific coast)
Days of rainfall: 6

JANUARY

Costa Rica in
SUMMER

Carrera Chirripó

Held on the last Saturday of February, Carrera Chirripó is an annual 21km footrace running up and down Cerro Chirripó, Costa Rica's highest peak.

📍Cerro Chirripó, p214

▶ carrerachirripo.com

↙ El Rezo del Niño

January 6 marks the end of the Christmas season. Families take down their nativities over food and prayer.

↗ Envision Festival

A seven-day festival of yoga, meditation, beach dance parties and concerts in Uvita with a sustainability focus. Usually begins in late February and ends in early March.

📍Uvita

▶ envisionfestival.com

FEBRUARY

Average daytime max: 27°C, 82°F (Pacific coast)
Days of rainfall: 2

Average daytime max: 28°C, 83°F (Pacific coast)
Days of rainfall: 2

🧳 Packing Notes

Pack your rain jacket, rain boots and an umbrella to be prepared for spontaneous storms.

Semana Santa

Holy Week, the week between Palm Sunday and Easter Sunday, is the busiest for domestic tourism, so popular destinations, especially beaches, are packed.

← National Boyero Day

A joyous caravan of colorful carts pulled by oxen takes place in the last two weeks of March in downtown Escazú.

📍 Escazú

Feria Orotina

The National Fruit Festival in Orotina, an hour from San José, celebrates local agriculture with open-air produce markets, a beauty pageant and sustainable farming workshops. It takes place in mid-March.

📍 Orotina

▶ facebook.com/FeriaOrotinaOfficial

← Turtle Nesting

Peak nesting season for turtles in Parque Nacional Tortuguero begins, with leatherback turtles setting it off.

📍 Parque Nacional Tortuguero, p90

MARCH

Average daytime max: 28°C, 83°F (Pacific coast)
Days of rainfall: 3

APRIL

Costa Rica in
AUTUMN

→ Día del Trabajador y la Trabajadora

International Workers Day, or Labor Day, is celebrated globally on May 1. In Costa Rica there are parades, marches and a 'State of the Union' address from the president in Limón City. It's also celebrated with cricket matches.

COSTA RICA PLAN BY SEASON

MAY

Average daytime max: 29°C, 84°F (Pacific coast)
Days of rainfall: 8

Average daytime max: 28°C, 83°F (Pacific coast)
Days of rainfall: 19

📋 Packing Notes

Be prepared for a mix of sun and clouds – always bring a hat and sunscreen, even if it's overcast.

Rainy season begins for much of the country.

← LGBTIQ+ Pride

Thousands gather for Costa Rica's largest parade celebrating LGBTIQ+ Pride in San José, usually on the last Saturday of June. Manuel Antonio also hosts smaller Pride parties and events.

📍 San José, p249

📍 Manuel Antonio, p249

International Festival for Peace

This festival features four days of singing by choirs from around the country and the world. Usually the last week of June.

Virgin of the Sea Day

Fishermen conduct a sea procession with decorated boats and pray for a fruitful year. On July 16 or the Saturday closest to that date.

📍 Puntarenas

JUNE

Average daytime max: 27°C, 82°F (Pacific coast)
Days of rainfall: 21

JULY

Costa Rica in

WINTER

← Whale-Watching

Peak humpback whale-watching season begins in July and lasts until November. Parque Nacional Marino Ballena and Bahía Drake are the best places to see them.

📍 Bahía Drake, p218

📍 Parque Nacional Marino Ballena, p199

Annexation of Guanacaste

This historical event is celebrated annually on July 25 with marimba music concerts, dancing and carnival rides.

→ Recognizing Afro-Costa Rican Culture

August 31 is Día de la Persona Negra y la Cultura Afrocostarricense. There are vibrant parades with dancers, bands and food stalls.

AUGUST

Average daytime max: 27°C, 82°F (Pacific coast)
Days of rainfall: 18

Average daytime max: 27°C, 82°F (Pacific coast)
Days of rainfall: 22

 Packing Notes

Pack your rain jacket, rain boots and an umbrella to be prepared for the rainy season.

September is the rainiest month for most of the country.

↓ Lantern Parade

On September 14, Ticos make homemade lanterns and parade with them around their neighborhoods to kick off Independence Day celebrations.

Dia de las Culturas

While honoring Columbus's colonization, it celebrates the mixing of immigrant and indigenous cultures. Occurs every October 12.

↑ Dia de la Independencia

Costa Rican Independence Day is on September 15. It honors Central America's independence from Spain in 1821. Festivities often start the night before.

SEPTEMBER

Average daytime max: 27°C, 82°F (Pacific coast)
Days of rainfall: 24

OCTOBER

Costa Rica in

SPRING

Limón Carnival

This 12-day celebration in Limón City commemorates Columbus's arrival with parades, calypso and dancing in the streets, food festivals and fireworks. It typically begins on October 12.

📍 Limón City

→ Dia de los Muertos

On November 1, families attend Catholic masses and make pilgrimages to cemeteries to honor their ancestors and loved ones who have passed away.

↖ Dia de la Mascarada

On Masquerade Day, October 31, locals make and wear elaborate papier-mâché masks depicting various characters, especially political and cultural figures or celebrities.

COSTA RICA PLAN BY SEASON

NOVEMBER

Average daytime max: 27°C, 82°F (Pacific coast)
Days of rainfall: 24

Average daytime max: 27°C, 82°F (Pacific coast)
Days of rainfall: 15

🧳 Packing Notes

Bring knee-high rain boots with solid traction to navigate muddy trails and deep puddles.

NORTHWEST COSTA RICA
Trip Builder

**TAKE YOUR PICK OF MUST-SEES
AND HIDDEN GEMS**

▬▬ Sample Costa Rica's biodiversity in one road trip. This loop starts and ends in San José, but takes travelers on a journey to waterfalls, volcanoes, a cloud forest and beaches.

🗺 Trip Notes

Hub towns San José, La Fortuna, Monteverde, Jacó

How long Allow 10 days

Getting around Rent a car from Juan Santamaría Airport (SJO) in San José

Tips Prepare for varying weather conditions and temperatures. Pack layers and a rain jacket, especially for Arenal evenings and cloud forest excursions. Take hiking boots for navigating waterfalls, volcanoes and cloud forests. Bring a bathing suit and water shoes for hot springs in La Fortuna and the beach in Jacó.

Santa Elena Cloud Forest Reserve
Experience one of Costa Rica's rarest ecosystems: the cloud forest. Meander along misty trails and lush paths among the clouds.
🚗 *20min from Monteverde*

Unión

Laguna de Arenal

El Castillo ○

○ Santa Elena

Monteverde ●

Guacimal ○

Rancho Grande ○

Golfo de Nicoya

Monteverde
Dine on local farm-to-table cuisine, and eat amid cloud forest flora and fauna at this foodie paradise.
🚗 *3hr from La Fortuna*

Península de Nicoya

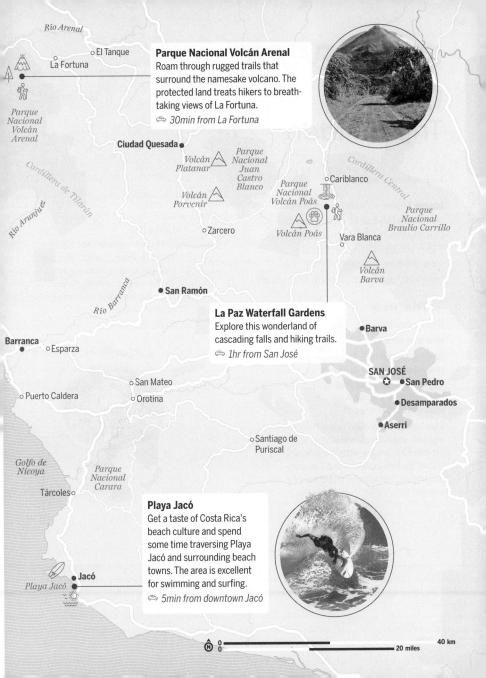

Río Arenal

El Tanque

La Fortuna

Parque
Nacional
Volcán
Arenal

Parque Nacional Volcán Arenal
Roam through rugged trails that surround the namesake volcano. The protected land treats hikers to breathtaking views of La Fortuna.

🚗 *30min from La Fortuna*

Ciudad Quesada

Volcán
Platanar

Parque
Nacional
Juan
Castro
Blanco

Cariblanco

Parque
Nacional
Volcán Poás

Cordillera Central

Volcán
Porvenir

Zarcero

Volcán Poás

Vara Blanca

Parque
Nacional
Braulio Carrillo

Cordillera de Tilarán

Río Arunjug

Volcán
Barva

Río Barranca

San Ramón

La Paz Waterfall Gardens
Explore this wonderland of cascading falls and hiking trails.

🚗 *1hr from San José*

Barva

Barranca

Esparza

SAN JOSÉ

San Pedro

San Mateo

Puerto Caldera

Orotina

Desamparados

Aserri

Santiago de
Puriscal

Golfo de
Nicoya

Parque
Nacional
Carara

Tárcoles

Playa Jacó
Get a taste of Costa Rica's beach culture and spend some time traversing Playa Jacó and surrounding beach towns. The area is excellent for swimming and surfing.

🚗 *5min from downtown Jacó*

Jacó

Playa Jacó

N

0
0

40 km

20 miles

CARIBBEAN COAST
Trip Builder

TAKE YOUR PICK OF MUST-SEES AND HIDDEN GEMS

▬▬▬ Home to Afro Costa Ricans and Bribrí indigenous communities, this region has a distinct Caribbean Tico culture. The coast has its own cuisine, music and surf vibe. Ecotourism adventures are abundant.

🗺 Trip Notes

Hub towns Limón City, Puerto Viejo

How long Allow 1 week

Getting around Save time by flying into Limón from San José. Rent a car in Limón City to explore Cahuita, Puerto Viejo and neighboring beach towns along the southern Caribbean coast.

Tips To visit Puerto Viejo by car, there's a one-lane coastal route and several one-car-at-a-time bridges. Avoid 'rush hour' (mornings 8am to 9am, afternoons 4pm to 5pm) and factor traffic into travel time.

Portete
Moín
Liverpool
Limón City

Río Babano

Limón City
Taste Limón's distinct Afro-Caribbean flavors at Jamaicatown's *sodas* (small local restaurants) and bakeries. Try the regional specialty, *rondon*, a delectable seafood soup with a coconut-milk base.
✈ *1hr flight from San José*

Río Telira

Río Coen

Parque Internacional La Amistad

Isla Uvita

Sail out to Isla Uvita for some of the Caribbean coast's best scuba diving. Experienced divers can explore an underwater shipwreck teeming with coral and all sorts of marine life.

⛴ *40min boat ride from Limón City*

Cahuita

Drive down the coast to Cahuita, home to the gorgeous Parque Nacional Cahuita. Visitors can hike trails along the beach and into the rainforest. Also check out the Cahuita Turtle Reserve.

🚗 *45min from Limón City*

Puerto Viejo & Playa Cocles

Surf bucket-list waves at these neighboring surf towns. But beware – many of them aren't for beginners! Salsa Brava, aka the 'Cheese Grater', beckons expert surfers, while Cocles is popular for surf lessons.

🚗 *30min from Cahuita*

Caribbean Sea

○ Pandora

Cahuita ●

Parque Nacional Cahuita

Puerto Viejo ●

Punta Uva ○

Manzanillo ●

Bribrí ○

Refugio de Vida Silvestre Gandoca-Manzanillo

Bratsi ○

Manzanillo

Check out the southernmost town on Costa Rica's Caribbean coast with low-key beaches and the Gandoca–Manzanillo Wildlife Refuge, which protects the many turtles that come to nest here.

🚗 *20min from Puerto Viejo*

PANAMA

Ⓝ 0⎯⎯⎯⎯⎯⎯⎯⎯⎯⎯ 20 km
   0⎯⎯⎯⎯⎯⎯⎯⎯⎯⎯ 10 miles

CENTRAL PACIFIC COAST
Trip Builder

TAKE YOUR PICK OF MUST-SEES AND HIDDEN GEMS

This route offers a delightful mix of lazy beach time, national park hikes, waterfalls and a mangrove tour into what *National Geographic* called the most 'biologically intense place on the planet.'

🗺 Trip Notes

Hub towns Dominical, Uvita, Palmar Norte

How long Allow 2 weeks

Getting around As with many routes in Costa Rica, having a 4WD will be your best means of getting around, especially if you want to roam at your leisure. However, there are buses traveling between Dominical, Uvita and Sierpe, and from these towns you can book nature tours.

Tip Visiting Bahía Drake is easiest and most fun via motorboat ferry.

Parque Nacional Manuel Antonio

Hike through Costa Rica's most popular national park to spy sloths, toucans and monkeys in their natural habitat. Stop for a swim at the park's gorgeous beaches.

🚗 *1hr drive from Dominical*

○ Quepos
△ ○ Manuel Antonio
● ☼ Savegre
Parque Nacional Manuel Antonio 🐾

PACIFIC OCEAN

Bahía Drake

Travel slowly through Bahía Drake's coastal and rural towns to appreciate the Península de Osa's unique biodiversity. A day trip to Parque Nacional Corcovado is a must.

🚗 + ⛴ *2hr from Palmar Norte*

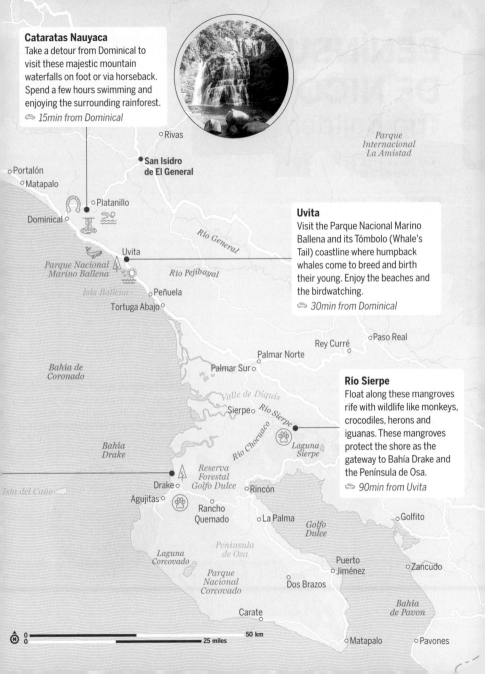

Cataratas Nauyaca

Take a detour from Dominical to visit these majestic mountain waterfalls on foot or via horseback. Spend a few hours swimming and enjoying the surrounding rainforest.

🚗 15min from Dominical

Uvita

Visit the Parque Nacional Marino Ballena and its Tómbolo (Whale's Tail) coastline where humpback whales come to breed and birth their young. Enjoy the beaches and the birdwatching.

🚗 30min from Dominical

Río Sierpe

Float along these mangroves rife with wildlife like monkeys, crocodiles, herons and iguanas. These mangroves protect the shore as the gateway to Bahía Drake and the Península de Osa.

🚗 90min from Uvita

Rivas

San Isidro de El General

Parque Internacional La Amistad

Portalón
Matapalo

Platanillo

Dominical

Río General

Uvita

Parque Nacional Marino Ballena

Río Pejibayal

Isla Ballena

Peñuela

Tortuga Abajo

Paso Real

Rey Curré

Palmar Norte

Palmar Sur

Bahía de Coronado

Valle de Diquís

Sierpe

Río Sierpe

Río Chocuaco

Laguna Sierpe

Bahía Drake

Reserva Forestal Golfo Dulce

Drake

Rincón

Isla del Caño

Agujitas

Rancho Quemado

La Palma

Golfo Dulce

Golfito

Zancudo

Península de Osa

Laguna Corcovado

Parque Nacional Corcovado

Puerto Jiménez

Dos Brazos

Bahía de Pavón

Carate

Matapalo

Pavones

N

0   50 km
0   25 miles

PENÍNSULA DE NICOYA
Trip Builder

TAKE YOUR PICK OF MUST-SEES AND HIDDEN GEMS

Explore some of Península de Nicoya's most famed beach towns. Surfers and sun worshippers will have endless options to enjoy the shore and the incredible sunsets on the Pacific coast. Share some time with Nicoya's resident sea turtles.

🗺️ Trip Notes

Hub towns Tamarindo, Nosara, Santa Teresa

How long Allow 2 weeks

Getting around A 4WD is necessary to navigate varying terrain, rough roads and river crossings.

Tips Fly directly into Liberia International Airport (LIR) for easy access to Península de Nicoya destinations. From there, you can catch direct flights to Tamarindo or Tambor, near Santa Teresa.

Parque Nacional Marino Las Baulas de Guanacaste

Matapalo ○ ○ Huacas

Beléno

Refugio Nacional de Tamarindo

Río Cañas

○ Villareal

Tamarindo

Santa Cruz ○

○ 27 de Abril

Paraíso ○

Parque Nacional Diriá

Marbella ○

● Nosara

Refugio Nacional de Vida Silvestre Ostional

○ Garza

Nosara
Witness thousands of sea turtles nest and hatch their eggs on these beautiful beaches. Visit the Refugio Nacional de Vida Silvestre Ostional to support these awesome creatures.

🚗 *2hr from Tamarindo*

Parque Nacional
Palo Verde

Reserva
Forestal
Taboga

Cordillera de Tilarán

Río Lagarto

Tamarindo
Get the party started in Tamarindo.
Surf some of the coast's sweetest
swells all day and then dance the
night away under the stars.
🚗 *2hr drive from LIR*

○ Guaitil

Parque Nacional
Barra Honda

Nicoya ○

Mansión ○

Río Nosara

○ Hojancha

Península
de Nicoya

○ Carmona

Jicaral ○

○ Lepanto

Playa
Naranjo

Isla
Caballo

Puntarenas ●

Isla San
Lucas

Golfo de
Nicoya

○ Santa Marta

Sámara
○ Carrillo

Sámara
Sunbathe and swim
in the gentle waves
at this family-friendly
beach. Surfers will
enjoy steady waves.
🚗 *1hr from Nosara*

○ Islita

○ Bejuco

La Javilla ○

San Francisco de Coyote

○ Paquera

Isla
Alcatraz

○ Pochote

○ Tambor

*PACIFIC
OCEAN*

Cóbano ○

Santa Teresa

Montezuma

Santa Teresa
Surf with some of the country's
prettiest people on some of the
prettiest beaches. Intermediate
and expert surfers have endless
entertainment.
🚗 *4hr from Nosara*

Mal País ○

○ Cabuya

Reserva Natural
Cabo Blanco

Montezuma
Hike through Península
de Nicoya's rainforest
for a day of swimming
in the epic falls. Three
different waterfalls and
pools offer something
refreshing for all types
of travelers.
🚗 *45min from Santa
Teresa*

0   0   20 miles   40 km

SOUTHERN COSTA RICA
Trip Builder

TAKE YOUR PICK OF MUST-SEES AND HIDDEN GEMS

▬▬▬ Rural ecotourism adventures await. Get to know Tico families and indigenous culture through homestays in remote and pristine landscapes. See rare quetzals, summit the country's highest peak and connect with its indigenous roots.

🗺 Trip Notes

Hub towns San José, San Isidro de El General, Buenos Aires, Palmar Norte

How long Allow 10 days

Getting around Rent a 4WD vehicle to access these outlying areas at your own pace.

Tips Download maps before leaving San José because cell service is spotty and wi-fi isn't readily available. This area has majestic mountain views but dangerous curvy roads, so drive cautiously. Fill up on gas and use ATMs in hub towns.

Santa María de Dota
Sip on some of the world's best coffee at CoopeDota, a coffee cooperative and plantation open for tours and tastings.

🚗 2½hr from San José

Santa Maria de Dot

Quepos
Manuel Antonio

Parque Nacional Manuel Antonio

Savegre

PACIFIC OCEAN

El Sitio Museo Finca 6
View the famous Disquis spheres created by Costa Rica's indigenous people centuries ago. Learn about their importance and connection to indigenous royalty.

🚗 30min from Palmar Norte

Providencia de Dota
See quetzals in their only Costa Rican habitat, the highlands of Providencia. Hike to hidden waterfalls in the highlands, and drink the country's best coffee, which is grown in the region.
🚗 *2hr from San José*

San Gerardo de Rivas
Ascend Cerro Chirripó, Costa Rica's highest peak, and spend the night among the clouds. Less experienced hikers can explore trails within the adjacent Cloudbridge Nature Reserve.
🚗 *30min from San Isidro de El General*

Térraba
Learn about the past and present of the indigenous Brörán and Boruca tribes on their ancestral land. Take a cacao tour, do mask-making workshops and stop by the Boruca Museum.
🚗 *2hr from San Isidro de El General*

Cañón

Parque Nacional Barbilla

Parque Nacional Tapantí-Macizo Cerro la Muerte
○ Ojo del Agua

Providencia de Dota
○ San Gerardo de Dota

Parque Nacional Chirripó

Parque Nacional Los Quetzales

Río Savegre

Herradura
San Gerardo de Rivas

△ *Cerro Ventisqueros*

San Isidro de El General ●

○ Rivas

Río Chirripó

Río Telira

Parque Internacional La Amistad

P A N A M A

○ Dominical
○ Escalares
○ Uvita

Parque Nacional Marino Ballena

Isla Ballena

○ Peñuela

Río General

Río Pejibayal

Buenos Aires

Río Cabagra

Parque Nacional Piedras Blancas

Térraba ●
🏛 Paso Real ○

Boruca ○

Bahía de Coronado

Palmar Norte
Palmar Sur ○ ● *Río Grande de Terraba*

Valle de Diquís
○ Sierpe

Río Sierpe
Chacarita

Laguna Sierpe

Bahía Drake

Isla del Caño

Drake ○ Rancho Quemado
Agujitas ○   ○ Rincón

Parque Nacional Corcovado

Península de Osa

Golfo Dulce

0
N 0
0

20 miles

40 km

7 Things to Know About
COSTA RICA

INSIDER TIPS TO HIT THE GROUND RUNNING

1 Pura Vida!

This phrase is ubiquitous, but not just for tourists. While it literally translates to 'pure life,' Ticos (as Costa Ricans refer to themselves) use the term in place of 'hello', 'goodbye', 'thank you' and 'you're welcome,' or to describe a laid-back or easygoing vibe.

2 Sodas

In Costa Rica a *soda* isn't a carbonated beverage, but rather a small local restaurant. Try a typical Costa Rican plate, known as a *casado*, which includes a meat choice (chicken, beef or fish), rice and black beans, a small salad, and sweet plantains. Some *sodas* make vegetarian versions if you ask. They're filling and relatively inexpensive compared to tourist restaurant prices.

3 Biodiversity

Remarkably, Costa Rica boasts 5% of the world's biodiversity. Unless you're staying in San José, you'll probably be up close and personal with nature.

4 It's Not Cheap

Costa Rica is the most expensive country in Central America. Travelers are often surprised at the cost of restaurants and hotels in particular. Budget accordingly.

5 Allow for Driving Time

Most highways outside of San José and Liberia (where the airports are) have only one lane in either direction. Many roads wind through mountains or traverse tricky terrain and require slow, patient driving and, depending on the season, *derrumbes* (landslides) sometimes block roads. There's also lots of construction to contend with in Costa Rica, which means traffic is often stopped and redirected.

Rent a 4WD for ease of travel over unpaved roads and, during rainy season, through creeks. Also, fill up on gas while passing through cities, since gas stations are sparse in remote areas.

Give yourself ample time and trust what Waze says. And then add time for food stops, bathroom breaks or scenic photos!

Download maps and routes while in wi-fi areas because in mountains and remote areas there may not be any connection.

6 Microclimates Aplenty

The weather can change drastically as you travel around the country. While much of the country has a tropical, humid and warm climate, the mountains and cloud forests can have chilly temperatures around 10°C. Areas like San Gerardo de Rivas, Providencia and Monteverde require a jacket and even hats or scarves depending on the time of year.

7 Dark by 6pm

Because Costa Rica is located so close to the equator, the sun rises and sets at approximately the same time every day regardless of the season. The sun is up around 5:30am and sets around 5:30pm, so by 6pm it's dark outside. When driving, plan to arrive earlier in the day to take advantage of the sunlight. It's harder, and more dangerous, to navigate remote locations and winding mountain roads when it's pitch black outside.

Read, Listen, Watch & Follow

 READ

"What Happen": A Folk-History of Costa Rica's Talamanca Coast (Paula Palmer, 1993) Afro-Costa Ricans preserving their culture.

Mo (Lara Ríos, 1992) Indigenous girl connects with the spirit world.

The Island of the Lonely Men (José León Sánchez, 1973) Fictionalized account of Sánchez's time imprisoned as an innocent man.

Única mirando al mar (Fernando Contreras Castro, 1993) Government treatment of the poor through the lens of environmental pollution.

 LISTEN

Manuel Obregón Musician, composer and former Minister of Culture who integrates nature and culture into his music.

Passiflora An all-women's group making self-described 'gypsy folk music' with ethereal genre-crossing grooves.

Walter 'Gavitt' Ferguson A Costa Rican calypso legend from the Caribbean coastal town of Cahuita.

Toledo One of the country's biggest reggae artists. Some of his music has a political slant, such as calling out police corruption.

KEVIN MAZUR/GETTY IMAGES ©

Debi Nova
A Grammy-nominated pop singer who has collaborated with Sergio Mendes, Q-Tip, Ricky Martin and more.

▷ **WATCH**

Maikol Yordan Traveling Lost (2014) Comedy about a farmer on a mission to save his land.

Caribe (2004) Drama about Caribbean banana farmers fighting land-grabbing oil corporations.

Endless Summer II (1994; pictured right) Documentary about local surf culture, particularly in Tamarindo.

Clara Sola (2021) A woman goes on a mystical journey to escape her repressive religious upbringing.

2.5% (2017) Documentary by Lokal Travel highlights Península de Osa and tourism's impact on its biodiversity.

NEW LINE CINEMA CINEMATIC COLLECTION/ALAMY STOCK PHOTO ®

○ **FOLLOW**

Two Weeks in Costa Rica
(twoweeksincostarica. com) Excursions resource, especially for families.

Descubre Costa Rica
(@descubrecostarica) Costa Rica bucket-list inspiration.

MyTanFeet
(mytanfeet.com) Travel tips and stories.

Caribeando
(@caribeandocr) Caribbean landscape and culture.

El Colectivo 506
(@elcolectivo506) Tico media organization focused on community journalism.

Sate your Costa Rica dreaming with a virtual vacation

SAN JOSÉ & THE CENTRAL VALLEY

CULTURE I CITY LIFE I DINING

Experience San José & the Central Valley online

AUTUMN SKY PHOTOGRAPHY SHUTTERSTOCK ©

Parque Nacional Juan Castro Blanco

Bajos del Toro

Parque Nacional Volcán Poás

Stroll among the enchanting hedge sculptures of **Parque Francisco Alvarado** (p58)
🚍 1½hrs from San José

○ Zarcero

Volcán Poás

Río Barranca

Reserva Forestal Grecia

○ Poasito

○ Vara Blanca

○ Concepción

● **San Ramón**

○ San Pedro de Poás

Palmares ○

Santa Bárbara

Learn about Costa Rica's singular war hero at the **Museo Histórico Cultural de Juan Santamaría** (p51)
🚌 *30mins from San José*

● **Alajuela**   **San Joaquín de Flores** ●

○ San Antonio

○ La Guácima

● **Santa Ana**

Escazú ●

SAN JOSÉ & THE CENTRAL VALLEY
Trip Builder

Zona Protectora Cerro de Escazú

Hike through mountainous coffee groves at **Hacienda La Chimba** (p55)
🚍 *20mins from San José*

▬▬▬ The Central Valley is the fertile crescent of Costa Rica. Enjoy spring-like weather, charming *pueblos* (small towns) and mountain ranges punctuated with volcanoes. In the middle lies San José, a diverse capital city jammed with museums and dining options.

Zona Protectora Caraigres

Santa Clara ○ ○ Guápiles

Walk right up to tumbling cascades at **La Paz Waterfall Gardens** (p55)
🚗 1½hrs from San José

△ Volcán Barva

Parque Nacional Braulio Carrillo

Río Sucio

Zona Protectora Acuíferos Guácimo y Pococí

Learn about pre-Columbian peoples at the **Museo del Jade** (p61)
🚌 In San José

Feast your eyes on the epic crater lake of **Volcán Irazú** (p68)
🚗 1½hrs from San José

Parque Nacional Volcán Turrialba

San Rafael ●

○ San Isidro de Heredia

△ Volcán Turrialba

● **Heredia**

San Juan de Tibas ●

San Isidoro de Coronado ●

Parque Nacional Volcán Irazú

🏛 **Guadalupe** ●

SAN JOSÉ ✪ ● **San Pedro**

Zona Protectora Río Tiribi

Revel amid rollercoasters, fireworks and a cowboy atmosphere at **Fiestas de Zapotes** (p62)
🚗 10mins from San José

● **Curridabat**

○ Pacayes

Alajuelita ●

Juan Viñas ○

Desamparados ●

Zona Protectora Cerros de la Carpintera

Río Reventazón

● **Cartago**

Take a scenic drive to the ruins and rainforest of **Lake Cachí** (p70)
🚗 1½hrs from San José

● **Paraíso**

Lago de Cachí ○ Cachí

Orosí ○

Río Navarro

Río Orosí

Tapantí

Zona Protectora Río Navarro-Río Sombrero

Parque Nacional Tapantí-Macizo Cerro la Muerte

FROM LEFT: ROBERT ISENBERG/LONELY PLANET ©, MIX TAPE/SHUTTERSTOCK ©, MICHAL SARAUER/SHUTTERSTOCK ©

Ⓝ 0 — 20 km
0 — 10 mile

Practicalities

MARCO LISSON/SHUTTERSTOCK ©

ARRIVING

Juan Santamaría Airport The busiest airport in Costa Rica, and the most direct route to the Central Valley. The airport is technically in Alajuela, a 25-minute drive from downtown San José. A crowd of *taxistas* (taxi drivers) will accost you at the terminal exit, and US$30 is a reasonable price for a metered ride into town. Walk a little further to the main road, and you can catch an express bus for US$1.50 or less.

HOW MUCH FOR A

Breakfast with *gallo pinto*
US$8

Gourmet coffee
US$2

Authentic Boruca mask
US$100

GETTING AROUND

Bus The Central Valley has a comprehensive bus system (p72), which is cheap (US$1 to US$1.50) and safe to ride. Routes can be confusing, but nearly all buses circle back to San José depots.

Taxi The default cab in San José is the *taxi rojo* (red taxi), which you can find almost anywhere. Make sure the *taxista* has a visible *maría* (meter). Rides around the inner city should cost between US$10 and US$30, depending on traffic.

Car Driving in the Central Valley can be a jaw-clenching thrill, and rental cars are affordable by US standards.

WHEN TO GO

NOV–JAN
Breezy, perfectly temperate, with possible showers

FEB–APR
Dry and hot, with clear skies and lots of crowds

MAY–JUL
Pleasant temperatures and afternoon rain

AUG–OCT
Humid but agreeable mornings followed by frequent thunderstorms

EATING & DRINKING

San José has the most dynamic dining scene in the country. True, you'll find a lot of familiar fast-food chains, plus windows selling cheap *empanadas* (turnovers stuffed with meat and cheese; pictured top right) and *arroz con pollo* (chicken rice). But the city is the best place to find Indian, Pan-Asian and South American cuisines, plus a range of chic gastropubs. You could spend days noshing your way through Barrio Escalante or Escazú. The options become more traditional in the smaller towns, but there's everything to love about a good *casado* (set meal; pictured bottom right).

Best craft-beer pub
Wilkcr (p66)

Must-try traditional meal
Nuestra Tierra (p74)

CONNECT & FIND YOUR WAY

Wi-fi SIM cards are widely available in the airport and city, and the biggest carriers are Claro and Kölbi. Free wi-fi (pronounced 'WEE-fee') is standard in hotels and guesthouses. Take the usual precautions installing cards and logging onto networks. You'll find less access in the mountains.

Navigation Ticos rely on the Waze app, preferring crowdsourced landmarks to street addresses.

MONEY

Cards are widely accepted, but it's wise to keep a small bundle of cash. Bus drivers carry boxes of exact change, so riding somewhere is a great way to break medium-value bills.

WHERE TO STAY

The city is packed with hotels of every budget and style. Small towns offer more boutique experiences. As a rule, prices are highest in the dry season.

Neighborhood	Pro/Con
Downtown San José	Museums and dining. Mixed quality. Withering crowds.
Barrio Escalante	Superlative accommodations and nightlife. Often sold out.
Escazú/ Santa Ana	Top-notch hotels. Family-friendly resorts. Often expensive and generic.
Alajuela	Near airport. Economical. Isolated and varying quality.
Heredia	Authentic town. Easy drive to sights and good access to Caribbean. Fewer options.
Orosí Valley	Beautiful landscape. Tourist-friendly. Very quiet.

SAFETY

San José can be rough around the edges, but the most common concerns are pickpockets and scammers. Men often try to catch women's attention with an annoying 'ts-ts-ts' sound, which is best ignored.

01 Park Yourself
HERE

OUTDOORS I SPORTS I ARTS

████ San José has lots of urban parks, but none of them compare to **La Sabana**. This sprawling greenspace is famous for its open fields and shady trees, and Ticos come from all over the city to jog or play ball. La Sabana served for 44 years as an international airport; today, the park helps urbanites escape San José's crowds and din.

JOSHUA TEN BRINK/SHUTTERSTOCK ©

🗺 How To

Getting here La Sabana is centrally located in San José and easy to reach by bus, taxi or foot. Parking can be a hassle, so reconsider driving.

When to go La Sabana is open all day, every day.

The outdoor facilities are best enjoyed when it's not raining, but there's always somebody on the turf.

Bring water There aren't a lot of water fountains or corner stores near La Sabana, so bring your own hydration.

ROBERT ISENBERG/LONELY PLANET ©

Top left Estadio Nacional **Bottom left** Museo del Arte Costarricense

Go solo La Sabana is covered in paths and walkways, so you can take a refreshing promenade through the trees or even run laps along the perimeter. The small 'lake' is surrounded by foliage and grass, making it the perfect spot for a picnic. There's also a public racetrack, and within the track is a rink for inline skating.

Join a team The park has several football fields, attracting players of all skill levels, and it's perfectly normal for random travelers to join a friendly game. The same goes for the baseball fields and volleyball court. There's even a small playground on the north side for the kiddos.

Browse the art One of the most beautiful buildings in San José is the **Museo del Arte Costarricense**, a former airport terminal built in traditional Spanish architectural style. It stands at the eastern entrance of La Sabana. Today, the structure serves as a museum with rotating art exhibits and historical retrospectives. The sculpture garden outside is a peaceful place to rest and regroup. The best part: admission is free.

Replenish calories La Sabana is lined with diverse restaurants, especially on the western side of the park. Pick from Asian, Mexican and South American menus. Two favorites are **Soda Tapia**, a popular diner with great breakfasts located near Paseo Colón, and **República Casa Cervecera**, a massive brewpub with classic bar fare and quality beers on tap.

🐽 Sports Capital

The **Estadio Nacional** (National Stadium) is considered the most modern in Central America, and the 35,000-seat venue is used for all kinds of major events. The stadium is best known as the home base of La Selección, Costa Rica's national football team, and international matches often take place here during the season. The field has also hosted regional matches and the Women's World Cup. Sports aside, the stadium serves as a main stage for some of the most famous musicians in the world; Shakira herself performed the first concert here in 2011, and big names perform here every month of the year.

02 War STORIES

HISTORY I MONUMENTS I MUSEUMS

▬▬▬ Costa Rica abolished its military on December 1, 1948, making it one of a few countries in the world without a standing army. Ticos were never warmongers, but traces of their martial past remain. Scattered monuments in Alajuela and Heredia are some of the most iconic of the Central Valley, both for their distinctive architecture and their significance to Costa Rica's formative years.

OLAF SPEIER/ALAMY STOCK PHOTO ©

📷 How To

Getting here Alajuela and Heredia are located near the airport. Scores of buses ferry passengers from San José to these cities and back, as do commuter trains. A taxi may be worthwhile as well.

When to go These landmarks are open most days, and they're worth visiting in any season.

Stay central All of the best sights in Alajuela and Heredia are within a couple of blocks of these central landmarks.

ROBERT ISENBERG/LONELY PLANET ©

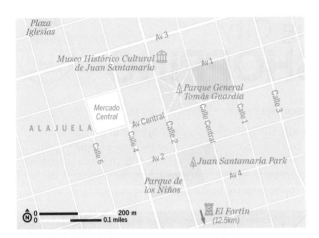

Plaza Iglesias

Av 3

Museo Histórico Cultural de Juan Santamaría

Av 1

Parque General Tomás Guardia

Calle 3

Mercado Central

Av Central

Calle 1

Calle Central

ALAJUELA

Calle 2

Calle 4

Calle 6

Av 2

Juan Santamaría Park

Av 4

Parque de los Niños

El Fortín (12.5km)

0   200 m
0   0.1 miles

Top left Juan Santamaria Park
Bottom left El Fortín

Hero's legacy Drummer boy Juan Santamaría was killed during a daring one-man assault on enemy lines in 1856. The **Museo Histórico Cultural de Juan Santamaría** transports visitors back to the Filibuster War, a bitter face-off between US mercenaries and Central American militias. Using dioramas and period artifacts, these exhibits explain the importance of Costa Rica's most celebrated war hero. The fortified structure has dominated Alajuela's downtown since 1895, adding to the museum's historical ambience.

Military monuments There aren't a lot of sword-waving statues in Costa Rica, thanks to its many years of peace, but you can find a significant few. **Juan Santamaría Park** is just a couple of blocks from the museum, where the young soldier's likeness is sculpted in bronze. The middle of Alajuela is marked by the **Parque General Tomás Guardia**, a busy plaza with a gazebo, fountain and statue of the bearded General Guardia, who twice served as president of 19th-century Costa Rica.

Towering achievement One of the most peculiar structures in Costa Rica is a former watchtower in the middle of Heredia called **El Fortín**. The stout brick cylinder and oval windows are unlike any other fortification from the 1870s, and the remaining three towers of the original plan were never completed. Today, El Fortín is the official symbol of Heredia, and visitors can enter the structure and view the town from its battlements.

Milestone Holidays

Costa Rica has several patriotic holidays, which recall major moments in the nation's history. Celebrations are biggest in the cities of the Central Valley, where thousands turn out to wave Costa Rican flags. The **Día de la Independencia** (September 15) commemorates Central America's hard-won secession from Spain in 1821 with parades across the country. During the **Día de Juan Santamaría** (April 1), the streets of Alajuela fill with marching bands in honor of their native son. In 2020, the government declared December 1 to be **Día de la Abolición de Ejército** (Abolition of the Army Day) to observe the many years of peace.

03 Big City **SHOPPING**

SHOPPING I WALKING I URBAN LIFE

███████ San José is a mercantile city, with thousands of brick-and-mortar stores competing for customers. You have myriad options for shopping in the big city, from a century-old bazaar to luxury retail developments. Whether you're looking for gifts for family or a replacement charger for your tablet, San José and its suburbs are the best place in the country to stock up.

🗺 **How To**

Getting around San José and Escazú are well connected by bus routes, and taxis are a great option for shorter distances.

When to go Indoor shopping is great all year, but outdoor malls should be avoided during rainy afternoons. Lots of merchants tend to close their shops on Sunday as well.

Cards are good Credit cards are widely accepted across San José, especially since the start of COVID-19.

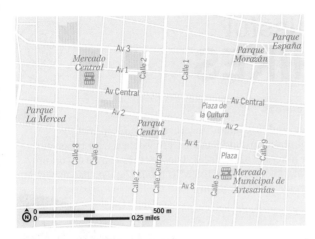

Top left Mercado Central **Bottom left** Chorreador and wooden decorative cart

Browse historic markets Vendors have sold their wares in the **Mercado Central** since 1880. This indoor complex has narrow walkways and a mishmash of shops and restaurants. You can find a lot of stock souvenirs here and easily score a cheap plate of *gallo pinto* (a rice and beans medley). A similar marketplace is the **Mercado Municipal de Artesanias**, where artists hustle to sell their crafts among densely packed stalls.

Hit the avenue The suburb of **Escazú** is a chic shopper's paradise, where plazas overflow with upmarket stores. The crème-de-la-crème is **Avenida Escazú**, a mixed-use development with high-rise condos, luxury chains and top-notch restaurants. The outdoor walkways are a spotless concourse along which you can while away an afternoon. For a more traditional experience, head down the road to **Multiplaza**, a massive indoor shopping mall.

Stroll pedestrian malls San José is a fairly walkable city, largely thanks to **Avenida Central** and **Avenida 4**. These two avenues run parallel to each other for almost a kilometer, and both are almost entirely blocked off to motor traffic. The brick walkways are lined on either side with clothiers, department stores and electronics depots. Shopping here can be a hit-or-miss experience, but the avenidas are a common place to start exploring San José, and the people-watching alone is worth a visit. For a bonus, check out a third pedestrian route, **Calle 9**, which runs perpendicular to them.

🏷 Traditional Gifts

You'll find lots of 'Pura Vida' bottle openers and Imperial T-shirts, but some souvenirs actually speak to Tico heritage. The **chorreador** is a traditional coffee maker made of wood and a cloth bag. **Boruca masks** are colorful wooden headwear in the likeness of demons, which are carved by the indigenous Boruca people for an annual festival. The **chonete** is a soft-brimmed hat commonly worn by Costa Rican farmers. **Hand-tooled leather** and **handmade wood products and pottery** make great gifts and may support local artists, although their origins are sometimes hard to verify. Finally, there's always the trusty bag of coffee.

04 Blissful **HIKES**

HIKES I WATERFALLS I VOLCANOES

▬▬▬ When you put 'valley' and 'highlands' together, you end up with spectacular views. The mountains around San José are webbed with trails, and a handful are designed for hikers of all abilities. These routes can be a workout, but they're also safe, well marked and close to civilization. You can also expect at least one breathtaking *mirador* (lookout point).

JURATEBUVIENE/SHUTTERSTOCK ©

🗺 How To

Getting here While it is possible to reach some of these trailheads by bus or taxi, a car is best.

When to go The dry season is best for all routes. During the rainy season,

try to hit the trail early in the day.

Reserve your spot For Volcán Poás, make sure to reserve with the **Sistema Nacional de Areas de Conservacion** (sinac.go.cr). For La Paz, also buy tickets in advance.

REBECA BOLANOS/SHUTTERSTOCK ©

Top left Volcán Poás Bottom left Hacienda La Chimba

Volcán Poás One of the most famous peaks in Costa Rica, Volcán Poás is a 2697m peak with a caldera, northwest of Alajuela. From the summit, you can gaze into an acidic lake and plumes of steam. The volcano has been so active in recent years that visitors are only allowed on the shorter trail, which takes about 10 minutes to hike from the parking lot. Helmets are required and available on-site.

Volcán Barva While it's far less dramatic than Poás, this volcano makes for a more satisfying hike. Barva is dormant, and the crater is filled with a lake and dense forest. Trails wind their way over the mountains, giving you unparalleled access to **Parque Nacional Braulio Carrillo**.

Mantra Trail In the hills above Santa Ana, **Hacienda La Chimba** is a sprawling coffee farm with ecotourism staples like ziplining and canopy tours. You can also hike the Mantra Trail, which takes you through the groves and past a succession of sculptures. The trail concludes with La Mano, a massive wicker hand that extends over the ridge.

La Paz Waterfall Gardens Thanks to five epic waterfalls, La Paz has become the most visited private preserve in Costa Rica. Trails and staircases have been cleverly constructed around the cascades, granting you a close-up view of the tumbling water. The La Paz property also contains animal displays and a luxury hotel.

🚲 Biker's Paradise

Mountain biking is all the rage in Costa Rica, and certain regions are crisscrossed with single-track trails. For a more curated experience, the Central Valley has several mountain-bike parks, where rated routes and constructed jumps cater to all skill levels. **Valle Escondido** is a playground for new and casual riders in suburban Santa Ana. In Heredia, **Adventure Park** provides epic alpine routes along with ziplining and canopy tours. **La Angelina** is a 40-hectare MTB park located between San José and Cartago, with 12 miles of trails and platforms. Note that none of these parks rent bikes, so make sure to bring one.

05 Animals Up **CLOSE**

WILDLIFE I ENVIRONMENT I ECOTOURISM

In a nation that boasts 5% of the world's biodiversity, *refugios* serve a double purpose: to help injured and abandoned animals, and to offer visitors an intimate encounter with native species. The Central Valley is hardly Costa Rica's wildest province, but a refuge is a safe place to see critters up-close before you seek them in their natural habitats.

TADAS_JUCYS/SHUTTERSTOCK ©

🗺 **How To**

Getting here Refuges in Escazú and Santa Ana are on established bus lines from San José. Locations in Alajuela and Heredia are easiest to reach by taxi or rental car.

When to go Each refuge has its own hours of operation. All have outdoor exhibits, so rain can be a factor.

Donations welcome If you're looking to support a good cause, note that most refuges work on a shoestring budget.

ONDREJ PROSICKY/SHUTTERSTOCK ©

Rescate Wildlife Center On the outskirts of downtown Alajuela, Rescate receives more than 2700 at-risk animals per year. A further 800 animals are on permanent exhibit, representing 125 species. Guests can walk the paved paths and see the gamut of wild cats, tapirs, monkeys and birds in a leafy setting. Covering 34 acres, the Wildlife Center is the largest sanctuary in the area.

Refugio Animal de Costa Rica This refuge is located on a twisty road between Escazú and Santa Ana, and more than 1500 individual creatures find their way to the facility each year. Visitors are required to take the 90-minute tour, which is led by a trained naturalist. After meeting crocs and white-faced capuchins, order some lunch at in-house restaurant **Croc's Comida Típica**.

Butterfly Kingdom Mariposario The organized tours at this butterfly preserve in Escazú are mostly designed for children and families, but honestly, who doesn't love butterflies? Learn about metamorphosis, migration patterns and the many butterfly species of Costa Rica while watching them flit around the small garden.

Toucan Rescue Ranch You'll find toucans, of course, but also sloths and barn owls. This ranch is headquartered in the hills of Heredia, where animals are rehabilitated and bred. If you can't find time to get here, the Rescue Ranch also hosts virtual tours.

Top left Keel-billed toucan **Bottom left** Zebra longwing butterfly

🖉 The Last Zoo

For the past century, people have come to the **Zoológico Simón Bolívar** to see exotic animals from around the world. The zoo has faced a lot of pressure in recent years, as Costa Rica moves toward a national policy of 'cage free' animals. To keep up with the times, the zoo now only displays species native to Costa Rica. If you find yourself in the Barrio Amón neighborhood of San José, you can visit this little zoo and its diverse collection of reptiles, mammals and birds. The zoo doubles as a botanical garden and often hosts kids' and cultural events.

06 Far-Out Art & FRESH AIR

PUBLIC ART I CHURCHES I SMALL TOWN

▬▬ Zarcero is a peaceful mountain town nestled in the highlands of Alajuela's coffee country. Locals love the rural landscape and year-long temperate weather. Travelers are drawn to two iconic landmarks: the spired church Iglesia de San Rafael and the fantastical topiary gardens of Parque Francisco Alvarado. Standing side-by-side, these creations are worth a pit stop on your way through the bucolic Central Valley.

🗺 How To

Getting here Take one of the regular buses from San José. If you're driving, make Zarcero part of a longer road trip through Alajuela.

When to go Zarcero is worth visiting any time of year, but mornings are best in the rainy season.

Stop and smell the hedges Many travelers beeline from San José to Arenal, but Zarcero makes for a relaxing place to spend the night.

Green art Zarcero is world-famous for its sculpted hedges, which have been shaped over the years into faces, animals and warped arches. These living monuments were the brainchild of artist Evangelista Blanco, who started to grow and shape the hedges in the 1960s. Visiting Parque Francisco Alvarado in the very center of town is like strolling through the pages of a playful children's book. You could easily spend an hour here admiring Blanco's patient workmanship, then grab a meal at one of Zacero's restaurants. Zarcero shows off the best of small-town life, and you can see the whole *pueblo* on foot.

Iglesia de San Rafael Above the park stand the twin spires of Zarcero's splendid central church. The red domes, central clock and double-staircased entrance look like something out of a storybook. Completed

🚗 On the Road in Alajuela

A popular road-trip is from San José to La Fortuna, which takes you through the rolling farmland of Alajuela Province, including Zarcero. There's a sameness to these little towns, but Alajuela has its worthy roadside attractions. The **Monumento Griego** is a pillared circle built in the style of a Classical temple. Visit the **Jardín Else Kientzler**, a botanical garden with more than 2000 tropical plant species. If you're passing through in January, **Palmares** is famous for its **Tope** (horse festival) when thousands of cowboys ride through the streets on their steeds.

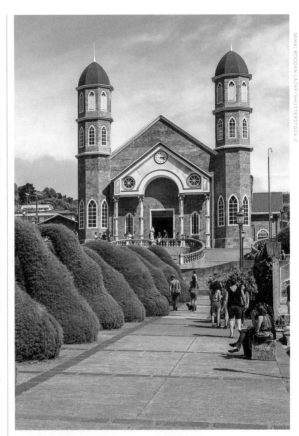

in 1895, the church is decorated with marble pillars and ornate New Testament paintings. A realistic painted sculpture of St Raphael clutching a fish welcomes visitors out front.

Stay over Thanks to its high elevation, Zarcero has one of the most coveted climates in Costa Rica. Most lodgings come in the form of chalets, *cabinas* (cabins) and bed-and-breakfasts, which are all cozy places to spend a cool night. A standout is the luxurious **Chayote Lodge**, about 15 minutes outside town in neighboring Naranjo. Chayote offers spacious suites and organizes a range of tours and activities.

Above Iglesia de San Rafael **Left** Sculpted hedges, Parque Francisco Alvarado

07 Capital
CULTURE

CITY I MUSEUMS I PERFORMING ARTS

San José is the cultural heart of Costa Rica, where world-class museums and cultural institutions await the curious traveler. This capital isn't known for beaches and biodiversity, but is a hotbed of artists, academics and entrepreneurs.

🗺 How To

Getting around
You can walk almost anywhere, and a *taxi rojo* (red taxi) is easy to spot. San José is also the hub for local and cross-country buses.

When to go San José is ready for you anytime.

Dress the part
Most *josefinos* wear trousers or dresses in this pleasant climate, and we advise sturdy shoes for weather-beaten sidewalks. Nothing says 'tourist' like shorts and sandals.

Pre-Columbian Museums

Two of the most impressive museums in Costa Rica stand only a few blocks from each other, and both explore the lives of indigenous peoples before the arrival of Europeans. The **Museo del Jade** displays stone carvings, ancient artifacts and elaborate dioramas of everyday tribal life. The enormous modern building is packed with sophisticated multimedia exhibits. The **Museo de Oro Precolombino** is an underground museum dedicated to the importance of gold to the early *caciques* (chiefs). See the many ways gold was used for dress, decoration and spiritual rites.

Live Music

Josefinos tend to have eclectic tastes in music: North American and European rock bands are huge here, and superstar vocalists from around

🏛 The Teatro Nacional

First opened in 1897, the Teatro Nacional is the historic flagship of San José's performing arts scene. Visitors can explore a small museum and grand auditorium, then order a beverage at the elegant **Alma de Café**. The theater remains as active as ever, holding performances large and small, for audiences of up to 1140 people.

Top left Museo de Oro Precolombino
Top right Teatro Nacional **Bottom left** Museo del Jade

the world make regular stops in San José. Better yet, the city has garnered a well-earned reputation for indie bands. **Amón Solar** is a converted house in the bohemian neighborhood of Barrio Amón, and you'll find everything from Latin to blues bands on its stage. **El Observatorio** is a brick-walled showroom in the party district of Barrio California. **StarView CR**, near Barrio Amón, has the feel of an underground bar from the 1990s, with music to match.

Arts Galore

San José has a good number of art galleries, which display experimental and avant-garde works you won't find anywhere else in Costa Rica. **TEOR/éTica**, in Barrio Amón, is an old corner building painted with a new mural every few months. In each room artists build installations that address social concerns. **Galería Talentum** is a sprawling 2nd-floor gallery housed in a former mansion from

☆ Fiestas de Zapote

Around the New Year, the **Fiestas de Zapote** commandeer this sleepy San José neighborhood, attracting thousands of families from across the valley. The streets are cordoned off to traffic, and you'll find the gamut of rollercoasters, sugary snacks and well-stocked beer-stalls. One of the major draws is the **Toros a la Tica**, Costa Rica's traditional rodeo, which takes place in the **Redondel de Zapote** (Zapote Arena). Nightfall brings festive lights and fireworks displays over the town. Travelers have about two weeks after Christmas to enjoy the ranching atmosphere. Cowboy hats are encouraged.

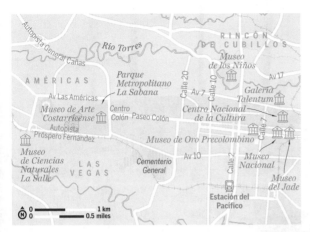

Left Fiestas de Zapote **Below** Museo de Ciencias Naturales La Salle

1902. The **Museo de Arte Costarricense**, in La Sabana Park, is in an elegant building constructed in a traditional Spanish style, with bleached white walls and tile roofs, making it hard to believe that the museum once served as an airport terminal.

Specialty Museums

The **Museo de los Niños** was once a prison, but today this jaunty yellow children's museum has castle-like towers and stands proudly on a hill. Inside you'll find dinosaur skeletons, science activities, an auditorium and even the **Galería Nacional**. In a similar vein, the **Museo Nacional** was once a military barracks, but today it looks like a fairytale palace in the middle of San José. Themed exhibits circulate through the museum on a regular basis, and the indoor butterfly garden is open year-round. Once a distillery, the **Centro Nacional de la Cultura** (CENAC) is a cluster of different buildings, including the **Museo de Arte y Diseño Contemporáneo** (Museum of Contemporary Art and Design) and **Teatro 1887**, which hosts a range of Spanish-language performing arts. Finally, in the southwestern corner of La Sabana Park, the **Museo de Ciencias Naturales La Salle** is a science museum packed with minerals and taxidermy animals.

08 Eat & Drink in
SAN JOSÉ

FOOD I BEVERAGE I NIGHTLIFE

San José is the epicenter of Costa Rican nightlife, where the dining options are most diverse and the bars stay open longest. Each neighborhood overflows with epicurean options, and places like Barrio Escalante and Escazú have garnered global attention for their dynamic nightlife.

How To

Getting around San José is walkable and well connected by buses, but if you're staying out late, taxis are a smart option.

When to go San José is always a happening city. Prices are best in the rainy season, but the city is most activated in the dryer months.

Plastic is golden In the wake of COVID-19, credit and debit cards are welcomed in most San José businesses.

Barrio Escalante

One of the most exciting places in San José is Barrio Escalante, where the culinary scene has exploded in recent years. The center of the action is **Calle 33**, a walkable street of cafes, restaurants and live entertainment. A good place to start is **Barrio Rojo**, an Edenic dining space with sumptuous entrees and craft cocktails. One of the oldest venues is still among the best: **Olio Restaurante** serves Mexican favorites in a cantina-like setting. Barrio Escalante is also full of guesthouses, making this neighborhood the easiest in San José to enjoy on foot.

Cerveza Artesanal

Costa Rica has fallen fully in love with *cerveza artesanal* (craft beer), giving Ticos far more options than the bottles of Imperial and Bavaria

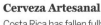

Classic Cinema

Movie buffs will get a kick out of **Cine Magaly**, a one-screen movie house in busy **Barrio California**. With its vintage marquee and diverse screenings, you can kick back with a bag of popcorn and catch flicks from all over the world. Magaly also participates in the multinational Shnit Film Festival.

Top left Calle 33 **Top right** Beer tasting
Bottom left Cine Magaly

stocked in every refrigerator. Gastropubs are everywhere in San José, inviting you to sample the many local beers and high-quality imports. One of the hippest bars in the city is **Stiefel Pub**, a two-story haunt with an exceptional beer list. You can also order creative pizzas, tacos, and other pub food in a youthful setting. The **Beer Factory** is an enormous Tyrollean *biergarten* located smack-dab in the middle of Barrio Escalante. A couple blocks down Calle 33 is **Wilkcr**, a bar with a slacker vibe, diverse brews and an entire wall covered with beer bottles.

Escazú

Swank Escazú is great for shopping and high-end service, but it positively excels at dining. The suburb is drenched in upscale restaurants, and you could spend weeks sampling them all. The real pride of Escazú is its global flavor: **Taj Mahal** is the best place in Costa Rica to find Indian cuisine, with Moghul-inspired decor. **La Divina Comida** serves Peruvian fare with masterful flavors and presentation. One of the hippest fusion

ⓘ San Pedro's College Scene

If you want to connect with a younger crowd, consider a night in **San Pedro**, home to the **Universidad de Costa Rica**. More than 40,000 students attend UCR, and most of them study, shop and party in San Pedro. You'll find a range of well-priced eateries, along with bookstores and specialty shops. UCR's grounds are open to the public, and you're welcome to frequent student cafes, visit the **Museo de Insectos** or gaze at the equatorial sky in the **Planetarium**. Come nightfall, head to **Calle de la Amargura**, a queue of throbbing nightclubs that spin dance music into the wee hours.

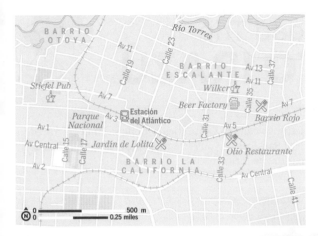

Left Blue morpho butterflies
Below Indian food

restaurants is **Tacobar**, where guests can build their own tacos out of an intricate salad bar. If you're not staying in Escazú, cars or taxis are the best transport.

Food Halls

The most exciting trend in local dining can be translated roughly as 'food hall.' In these communal settings, tiny restaurants are packed together and seating is shared. Patrons can order from one or several different windows and sit wherever they want. In Barrio Escalante, **Jardín de Lolita** describes itself as a 'gastronomic community,' and that feel-good vibe pervades the industrial space and verdant decor. You can pick from nine different eateries with fare from Mexican to Japanese. Lolita's central location makes it a natural choice for backpackers. Over in Santa Ana, **Container Platz** is a colorful construct made of repurposed shipping containers. Patrons can pick and choose from 17 different eateries, and specialties include burgers, poké bowls and fine Italian. Container Platz takes pride in being pet-friendly, and it's become one of the best spots in Santa Ana for DJs and karaoke nights.

09 Road Trip
TO IRAZÚ

DRIVE I VOLCANO I HISTORY

▬▬▬ Irazú is the tallest active volcano in Costa Rica, and its summit (pictured below) is within easy reach of San José. If you're renting a car, turn your Irazú visit into a road trip through the historic province of Cartago.

MICHAL SARAUER/SHUTTERSTOCK ©

🗺 Trip Notes

Getting around Cartago is a hub for buses, and downtown Cartago is very walkable. But a car is the only practical way to hit all five stops.

When to go Irazú is best in the mornings, when skies are clear. The rainy season can get especially foggy.

Reserve ahead Visitors to Irazú must reserve in advance with the **Sistema Nacional de Areas de Conservación** (sinac.go.cr).

🚶 Cartago Pilgrimage

For 250 years, Cartago was the capital of Costa Rica. Earthquakes and national politics have undermined Cartago over the years, but the city still wields a symbolic power. **La Romería**, a cross-country walk to the city's basilica, draws more than a million pilgrims to the historic downtown each summer.

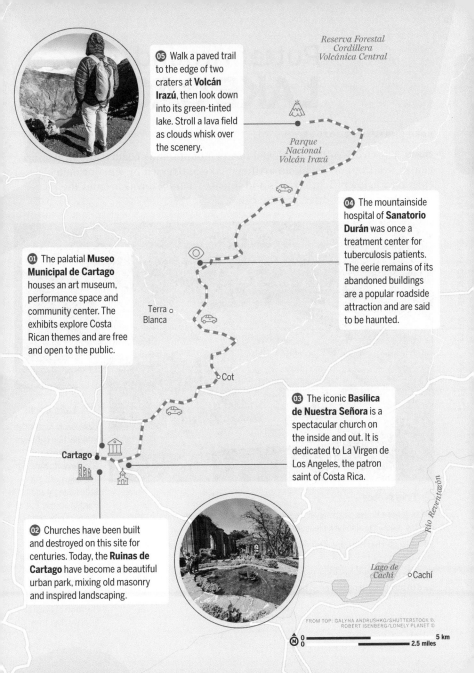

05 Walk a paved trail to the edge of two craters at **Volcán Irazú**, then look down into its green-tinted lake. Stroll a lava field as clouds whisk over the scenery.

Reserva Forestal Cordillera Volcánica Central

Parque Nacional Volcán Irazú

04 The mountainside hospital of **Sanatorio Durán** was once a treatment center for tuberculosis patients. The eerie remains of its abandoned buildings are a popular roadside attraction and are said to be haunted.

01 The palatial **Museo Municipal de Cartago** houses an art museum, performance space and community center. The exhibits explore Costa Rican themes and are free and open to the public.

Terra Blanca

Cot

03 The iconic **Basílica de Nuestra Señora** is a spectacular church on the inside and out. It is dedicated to La Virgen de Los Angeles, the patron saint of Costa Rica.

Cartago

Río Reventazón

02 Churches have been built and destroyed on this site for centuries. Today, the **Ruinas de Cartago** have become a beautiful urban park, mixing old masonry and inspired landscaping.

Lago de Cachí Cachí

N 0 — 5 km
0 — 2.5 miles

10 Putter Around LAKE CACHÍ

LAKE I NATURE I ECOTOURISM

The Orosí Valley is beloved for its mountainous beauty, and at its center lies Lago de Cachí, an artificial lake buttressed by a major dam (pictured below). Gentle roads and tourist-friendly towns around the lake make for a blissful drive or bike ride.

KRYSSIA CAMPOS/GETTY IMAGES ©

Trip Notes

Getting here Buses pass daily between Cartago and local towns. These gently curving roads can also be a pleasure to drive.

When to go The rivers are strongest in the rainy season, but landslides are also possible.

Early to bed Most businesses in the Orosí Valley are closed by 9pm, so make sure to buy everything you need before then.

Lake Cachí

Lake Cachí marks the intersection between the **Río Orosí** and **Río Reventazón**. The lake itself is a little swampy and hard to access, but the dam provides clean electricity to the valley, and the rivers are popular for fishing and whitewater rafting. Several tour companies in the town of Orosí can arrange river trips.

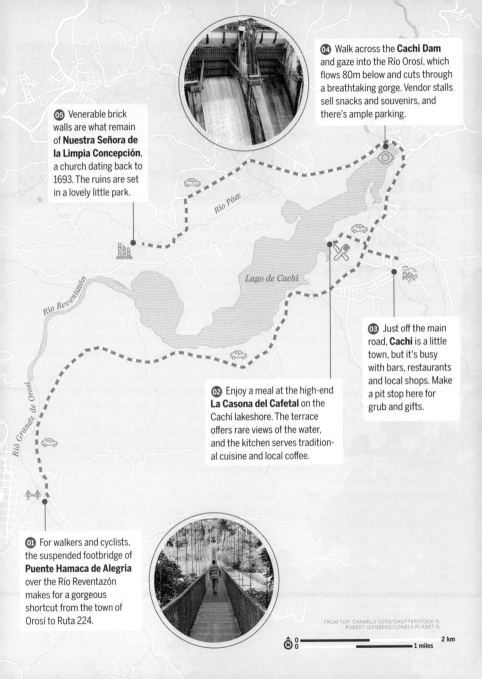

04 Walk across the **Cachí Dam** and gaze into the Río Orosí, which flows 80m below and cuts through a breathtaking gorge. Vendor stalls sell snacks and souvenirs, and there's ample parking.

05 Venerable brick walls are what remain of **Nuestra Señora de la Limpia Concepción**, a church dating back to 1693. The ruins are set in a lovely little park.

Río Páez

Lago de Cachí

Río Reventazón

03 Just off the main road, **Cachí** is a little town, but it's busy with bars, restaurants and local shops. Make a pit stop here for grub and gifts.

02 Enjoy a meal at the high-end **La Casona del Cafetal** on the Cachí lakeshore. The terrace offers rare views of the water, and the kitchen serves traditional cuisine and local coffee.

Río Grande de Orosí

01 For walkers and cyclists, the suspended footbridge of **Puente Hamaca de Alegría** over the Río Reventazón makes for a gorgeous shortcut from the town of Orosí to Ruta 224.

FROM TOP: CARMELA SOTO/SHUTTERSTOCK ©; ROBERT ISENBERG/LONELY PLANET ©

N
0   2 km
0   1 miles

To Bus or Not to Bus?

YOU CAN GET THERE FROM HERE

How you get around Costa Rica will determine how you interact with it. A cross-country bus can be sublime and economical – the ideal choice for first-time visitors. But there are benefits to driving, despite the many roadblocks you may encounter along the way. The best option may be a mix of both.

The Beauty of Buses

The seats are soft, the riders are quiet and cool air eases through open windows. All around, the tropical countryside reveals itself, the forests and farms, the mountains and rivers. You have nothing to do for the next couple of hours but watch the scrolling scenery and maybe take a siesta. If you don't mind mass transit, the Costa Rican bus is about as good as it gets. And it's cheap.

For years, backpackers have zigzagged across the landscape by bus, rarely paying as much as US$20 to cross entire provinces. These roads can be rough and full of switchbacks, even in the city; swallow a little Dramamine and let a professional driver take the wheel. This is the way most Ticos travel, and riders tend to be courteous and keep to themselves.

The vast majority of these buses end up in San José, the nation's transportation super-hub. City buses travel to every barrio and suburb, usually costing a dollar or less. Long-distance buses can take you to the Caribbean, the Pacific, volcanoes, national parks and almost any major town. The bus is a great option for travelers on a budget, and you can usually stow extra luggage in a handy undercarriage compartment. It's romantic and carefree, and you'll meet a lot more locals this way.

The 4WD Advantage

The Costa Rican bus system has its flaws, of course. For starters, there is no central terminal in San José, but rather several different stations and services, which are

Top left La Suiza **Top center** Cariari bus station **Top right** River crossing near Drake

generally located in dodgy neighborhoods. Depots can be grimy and full of characters, especially in the darker hours.

The main drawback is the bus' range of movement. Costa Rica is full of secret nooks, which are often impossible to reach without four-wheel-drive. Renting a car is vastly more expensive than the bus, and you do risk fender benders and mud traps. But you can also take control of your route, grinding over rocky roads to a little-known beach or waterfall. Such nooks can be just too far to trudge on foot, and you may find yourself rolling the dice on a taxi.

> For years, backpackers have zigzagged across the landscape by bus, rarely paying as much as US$20 to cross entire provinces.

The Best of Both Worlds

If you're wrestling with your budget, the most rewarding option is to bus for a while, get a sense of what you'd like to see, and then rent a car for a couple of days and double-back to all the spots you've missed. Costa Rica is geographically complex, and it's often hard to gauge travel time before you arrive. The bus will help you understand what you're dealing with, from road conditions to micro-climates. You'll figure out which neighborhoods in San José are worth fighting all that traffic. If all goes well, you'll put your time, and mileage, to good use – and probably hear about a dozen more sights for your next trip.

Hit the Rails

The most overlooked transport in the Central Valley is the commuter train, which can carry you to several major towns for a pittance. Its central hub is the humble **Estación Atlántico** in downtown San José, where passengers gather on the platform each morning and afternoon. The train is a little rickety, but it can take you all the way from Alajuela or Heredia to San José, and then beyond to Cartago. The 32-station system is the last remnant of a defunct national railroad network, and its wide windows offer unique vistas of the urban landscape.

The City & the Country

A JET-SETTING NATION, A HUMBLE PAST

Five-star restaurants. Luxury condos. Billboards advertising jewelry and electronics. San José is a 21st-century boomtown, and signs of its success are everywhere. But this image contrasts sharply with Costa Rica's agrarian roots. As Central Valley development amps up, we must remember what makes Ticos special: their connection to the land.

Top left Estadio Nacional **Top center** Casado **Top right** Catedral Metropolitana

In the middle of San José, you'll see the colorful facade of **Restaurante Nuestra Tierra**. Sculptures of a woman and man, dressed in traditional costume, stand next to the entryway. The tables are designed to look like rustic wood. Eating a meal here is like a tutorial on Costa Rican cuisine, from brothy *olla de carne* (pot roast) to *gallo pinto* (blended rice and beans) served on banana leaves. Even coffee is steeped in the canvas sock of an old-fashioned *chorreador*. Nuestra Tierra means Our Land, and the restaurant doubles as a monument to Costa Rican pride. Across from the Plaza de la Democracia, on one of downtown's busiest roads, Nuestra Tierra is an idyllic getaway of wagon wheels and woven baskets. The easygoing dining room contrasts sharply with the diesel fumes and panhandlers just outside.

Costa Rica has changed rapidly in the past few decades. As recently as the 1980s, outsiders perceived this country as a sleepy Central American backwater, known mostly to intrepid backpackers with a high tolerance for rutted jungle roads. Since then, ecotourism has exploded and San José has rapidly modernized. Suburbs have sprung up between disparate towns, and sprawl extends for miles in every direction. The capital is full of cultural institutions, from the historic **Catedral Metropolitana** to the state-of-the-art **Estadio Nacional**. San José has become a city of entrepreneurs, restaurateurs, hoteliers and nonprofit founders. Three-quarters of Costa Rica's population now live in the Central Valley, among them thousands of expats.

Still, the soul of Costa Rica is in its *campo* (countryside). The nation's economy first prospered because of its fertile volcanic soil. Today, urbanites flee to the beaches and

mountains every weekend. Family remains the strongest bond, and even the hippest city slickers make time to gather with their kin for dinner. The preferred meal is still some variation of rice and beans, the same staples eaten by farmers for generations. Tico humor has always been bawdy and down-to-earth. These are folks who love simplicity, who don't like to rush things. You won't find a lot of hoarders here; most people only have enough possessions to furnish their homes.

The farther you venture from the city, the more relaxed the people seem. In the small *pueblos* of the Central Valley, locals wave to strangers and help with directions. '*Pura vida*' isn't just a phrase, but a way of life. The government may have disbanded the army in San José, but the passion for living in peace is the hallmark of the *campesino*. The same goes for environmental stewardship; farmers carefully tended the fields long before the first carbon-neutral resort.

Nuestra Tierra is a sentimental restaurant, but it also reminds visitors of those agrarian roots. Costa Rica had embraced its new roles as global playground and environmental champion, and Ticos should be proud of all they have accomplished. But, as many Ticos have observed, '*Costa Rica es un pueblo*.' You could translate this two ways: 'Costa Rica is a small town,' or 'Costa Rica is one people.'

> The soul of Costa Rica is in its *campo* (countryside). The nation's economy first prospered because of its fertile volcanic soil.

ⓘ **Scenes Frozen in Time**

What did Costa Rica look like before all the highways and radio towers? How did Ticos dress and get through their days, back in the era of oxcarts and mule paths? Archival photos can be helpful, but a more vivid portrait is the **Museo Histórico Agrícola** (Farm History Museum) in Santa Ana. Based in the **Centro de Conservación**, the museum is an actual antique farm full of retro tools and machinery from the early 20th century. You can also check out the traditional farm in the middle of **La Paz Waterfall Gardens**, where a *cabina* (cabin) and barn have been lovingly recreated.

THE VALLEY
at a Glance

01 Chifrijo
No San José pub crawl is complete without this hearty stew of *frijoles* (beans) and *chicharrones* (pork rinds).

02 Museo Nacional
This castle-like facade (p63) is easy to spot in downtown San José, and exhibits include art galleries and a butterfly garden.

03 Juan Santamaría
This bronze statue (p51) in Alajuela honors Costa Rica's only major war hero, who died on a daring one-man raid.

04 Las Esféras
These mysterious stone orbs are attributed to pre-Columbian peoples. Original spheres and facsimiles decorate major buildings, including the Estadio Nacional.

05 Estadio Nacional
This 35,000-seat sports complex (p49) is the envy of Central America and home to La Selección, Costa Rica's soccer team.

06 Guaro
This clear liquor is made from sugarcane. Cacique Guaro distills the national spirit, which mixes well with anything.

07 Central clock
An ornate clock and fountain stand on the edge of the Plaza de la Cultura, marking a common rendezvous point.

08 Taxi rojo
Hail a *taxi rojo* (red taxi) just about anywhere in the Central Valley to quickly zip to your destination.

09 El Fortín
This distinctive lookout tower (p51) was once part of a colonial fort. and is now the proud symbol of Heredia.

Listings

BEST OF THE REST

Food Halls

La Fortina Mercado Gastronómico $$

Sample two stories of global flavors in the heart of Heredia. Named after the city's famous tower, family-friendly La Fortina has its own parking lot and regular live bands.

Calle 33 $$

This Escazú hotspot takes its name from the neighborhood's busiest corridor. Browse 10 windows for tacos, ramen or ceviche, then settle on a pet-friendly patio.

Jardín de Lolita $$

Polished picnic tables, strung-up lights and more styles of cuisine than you could try in a single night. This edenic food hall in Barrio Escalante serves everything from sushi to burgers.

Container Platz $$

Shipping containers make for cool architecture, especially when each contains a different mini-restaurant. Mosey over to Santa Ana for wraps, ice cream or poké bowls.

The Box CR $$

Escazú wouldn't be complete without its modernist horseshoe full of restaurants. The Box feels more like a shopping plaza, but it's still easy to try several places in one visit.

El Mestizo $$$

In the commercial sprawl of Escazú, El Mestizo Mercado Gastronómico is a flavor oasis. Morning waffles, noontime tapas and a full night at the biergarten.

Unique Stays

Gran Hotel Costa Rica

This handsome hotel from the 1930s stands next to San José's Plaza de la Cultura. The hotel was recently renovated but retains its vintage ambience. Notable guests include John F Kennedy.

URBN Escalante

This 29-story apartment complex towers over Barrio Escalante in San José. Many tenants rent their apartments to guests, who enjoy a rooftop pool and one of the best views in the city.

Peace Lodge

The La Paz estate in Alajuela is best known for its waterfall gardens, but you can also stay the night, giving you time to savor the on-site restaurants and animal sanctuaries.

Xandari Resort & Spa

Drive 15 minutes north of Alajuela and find lush countryside, expansive verandas and all the wellness treatments you could hope for. Easy access to the airport makes this a pampering vacation-ender.

Peace Lodge, La Paz Waterfall Gardens

Finca 360

It doesn't look like a farm, but the 360-degree views are soul-stirring. With only five rooms, this mountainside lodging in rural Alajuela offers a spa, a kitchen and yoga sessions.

 Cultural Encounters

Mercado Central

Browse among the same stalls where Ticos have done their shopping for generations. Hundreds of vendors sell everything from spinach to handbags in this feisty indoor environment.

Teatro Melico Salazar

You might walk right by this hallowed auditorium in downtown San José, but don't let it's bland facade deceive you: professional concerts, theater and dance all take place on its stage.

Antigua Aduana

Once a customs house, this voluminous brick building on the edge of Barrio Escalante holds large-scale cultural events. Expect to walk into a concert or craft market any given day.

Teatro Luciérnaga

This beautiful new theater occupies the 2nd floor of a shopping complex in Umara, just south of the city. Catch quality musicals and cabarets straight out of the Broadway songbook.

Ojo de Agua

This easygoing Alajuela water park is named after its eye-shaped fountain. These pools are a favorite among Ticos and cheap to visit. Still, you'll rarely find another traveler in the place.

Parque Diversiones

For old-school rollercoasters, you can't do better than Parque Diversiones in Alajuela. Founded to fund the Hospital de los Niños, this amusement park is entertaining for all ages.

ROBERT ISENBERG/LONELY PLANET ©

Ojo de Agua

SAN JOSÉ & THE CENTRAL VALLEY REVIEWS

Sibö Chocolate

This little chocolate company in Heredia celebrates Costa Rica's underrated cacao industry. Learn about the history of chocolate in its hilltop location, or visit the second shop and cafe in Escazú.

Museo Histórico Cultural de Juan Santamaría

This museum in downtown Alajuela celebrates Costa Rica's role in the Filibuster War of the early 19th century. It's also close to the Mercado Municipal, a historic indoor bazaar.

Casa de la Cultura Alfredo Gonzáles Flores

This vintage house in downtown Heredia is located right next to El Fortín and curates both gallery shows and lecture series. A permanent exhibit honors historic Costa Rican president 'Don Alfredo.'

Monumento Nacional Guayabo

This pre-Columbian town mysteriously thrived several hundred years ago, but no one knows who built it or why its society disbanded. Hike around this well-excavated archaeological site.

Hacienda Orosí Hot Springs and Farm

Come for the hot springs, stay for the crash-course in agriculture. Laze in Hacienda Orosí's five thermal pools, dine in its upscale restaurant and take a farm tour.

🏛 Sacred Sites

Catedral Metropolitana

The cathedral is a colossal church in San José, standing on one end of the Parque Central. This is also the site for a recreated crucifixion scene during Holy Week.

Tres Cruces Trail

This rigorous hike in the mountains above Escazú is no task for beginners, but climbers will be rewarded with divine views – plus three crucifixes scattered across the peaks.

Parroquia San Antonio de Padua

This red-roofed church in Escazú yields a divine view of the Central Valley. It's also nestled in the middle of town, next to an attractive flower garden.

Iglesia de Santa Ana

This historic church is an anchorpoint in the middle of Santa Ana. Admire its simple stone architecture, then come back on Sunday for the weekly farmers' market just outside.

Parroquia Vázquez de Coronado

No church in Costa Rica looks more like it was transported directly from the French countryside. This church in Coronado is a gothic masterpiece, although it was notably finished in 1930.

Basílica de Nuestra Señora de los Ángeles

The magnificent basilica in the middle of Cartago is an active church, but it's also a destination for pilgrimage. See 'La Negrita,' a carved stone with a miraculous 17th-century past.

Iglesia Colonial de Orosí

This simple church across from Orosí soccer field is considered the oldest Costa Rican church to hold continuous services, having survived earthquakes and social tumult. Visit the adjacent museum to learn more.

☕ Coffee Experiences

Cafeoteca

This bright former ranch house has a spacious atrium and sophisticated local coffees. Cafeoteca was a pioneer in Barrio Escalante, where many similar high-end cafes have sprung up.

Britt Coffee Tour

Local coffee giant Britt has its headquarters in Heredia, where visitors can join a multimedia plantation tour, savor a cappuccino in the open-air cafe and browse the coffee-scented gift shop.

Hacienda La Chimba

In the hills above Santa Ana, Hacienda La Chimba hosts coffee tours plus dinners in its restaurant. Make a day of it with ziplining, ropes courses and independent hiking.

Hacienda Alsacia

Best known as a Starbucks supplier, Hacienda Alsacia in rural Heredia offers a compelling tour for a well known product. Stop here on the way to or from Volcán Poás.

Finca Rosa Blanca

You may love visiting the Finca Rose Blanca farm so much, you'll want to stay over. Luckily, the *finca* doubles as a boutique hotel, with jaw-droppingly beautiful accommodations and surroundings.

Basílica de Nuestra Señora de los Ángeles

🍷 Grab a Drink

El Cuartel $$

In the throbbing Barrio California party district of San José, El Cuartel is a cozy, old-school tavern. Order from a classic bar menu, swig an Imperial and catch a match.

Mandrágora $$

This Barrio Escalante gastropub is modeled on the Harry Potter franchise, complete with robed servers, entrees named after characters, and 'broomstick parking' outside. The cocktails work magic.

LA Buenos Aires $$

This is your classic San José pub with a long, L-shaped bar. Located next to Santa Taresita Church, LA Buenos Aires has a long history of wedding after-parties.

Café Los Deseos $$

Romantic lighting and superlative pub food make this place a must-visit in Barrio Carmen. Come for the artful decor, stay for the margaritas thick with chopped fruit.

Club Alemán $$

The German Club is popular among Central European travelers, but all are welcome. The food is meaty and well prepared, and there's no better place to celebrate Oktoberfest.

Soberanos $$

The first thing you'll see is a big porch and cartoon cats painted on the facade. Step inside this Escalante pub for burgers, noodle bowls and a discriminating beer selection.

La Criollita $$

The classic San José restaurant has white tablecloths, framed paintings and a lively little bar. Professionals often come here after work, and the menu lives up to its 'Creole' namesake.

Hacienda La Chimba

Central Pub $$

Just a stone's throw from La Sabana Park, step into the English-style pub for inventive cocktails and live music in the adjacent London Room.

Jazz Café $$

Tucked into an Escazú frontage road, Jazz Café is a state-of-the-art performance venue drawing some of the best musicians in Costa Rica. Expect energetic concerts and expert cocktails.

Bar Chubbs $$

Chubbs is an archetypal American sports bar, with Buffalo wings, buckets of beer and global sports on TV. When you're in Escazú and need the 'Cheers' experience, hit up Chubbs.

República Casa Cervecera $$

A voluminous brewpub next to La Sabana Park, Republica Casa showcases brightly colored taps and crispy fish and chips. The beer and festive atmosphere make this a major hotspot.

Scan to find more things to do in San José & the Central Valley online

CARIBBEAN COAST

NATURE | HISTORY | ADVENTURE

Experience
the
Caribbean
Coast online

CARIBBEAN COAST
Trip Builder

El Caribe's vibe is like nothing else in Costa Rica: part Tico, part Rastafarian, part Jamaican, with fusion spins on classic dishes, stunning beaches and jungle, and lively, historically relevant big cities that reveal fantastic art and culinary scenes if you peek below the surface.

Caribbean Sea

Parque Nacional Tortuguero

Caño Blanco○

Snorkel **Isla Uvita**, Limón's unin-habited snorkeling paradise (p88)
⛴ *40min from Limón City*

Marvel at the traditional water-enveloped village of **Parismina** (p106)
🚆 + ⛴ *90min from Siquirres*

Portete○

Parque Nacional Barbilla

Liverpool○   ▣ **Limón City**

○Turrialba

○Tuis   ○ Bomba

Parque Nacional Cahuita

Tackle apex-level surfing at **Salsa Brava** in Puerto Viejo (p86)
🚶 *3min from central Puerto Viejo*

Explore hidden waterfalls and clandestine tidal pools at **Cahuita** (p98)
🚗 *10min from Cahuita*

Pandora○

Puerto Viejo ◉   Punta Uva

Bribrí○

Observe the leatherback nesting ground at **Manzanillo** (p102)
🚶 *20min guided walk from Manzanillo*

Cordillera de Talamanca   *Río Telira*

Bratsi○

Parque Nacional Chirripó

Sixaola○

P A N A M A

Visit Puerto Viejo's cultural and community hub, **Casa de la Cultura** (p96)
🚶 *5min from central Puerto Viejo*

DAMSEA/SHUTTERSTOCK ©

Practicalities

ARRIVING

Fly into San Jose's **Juan Santamaría International Airport** and take the direct bus to Limon, or fly to **Limon International Airport** and take a six-minute taxi ride into the city.

MONEY

Eat at local *sodas* (small local restaurants) and stay at homestays to save cash. Don't expect good wi-fi at budget options.

CONNECT

Wi-fi tends to be spotty in remote places in El Caribe, so it's a smart idea to have an international plan or get a local SIM card.

WHERE TO STAY

City/Town	Pro/Con
Puerto Viejo	Excellent nightlife, accommodations for every budget. Better nature elsewhere.
Limón City	Great food, amazing history. Difficult to navigate.
Cahuita	Amazing music scene. Fewer amenities.
Manzanillo	Tons of nature and animals. Little nightlife.

EATING & DRINKING

El Caribe's cuisine is Jamaican influenced. As such, you'll find traditional rice and beans served with coconut milk, jerk-style dishes (pictured top left), garlic potatoes, *patis* (small savory pastries), and Caribbean-influenced sweets like yucca rolls (pictured bottom left) and ginger biscuits. People on the Caribbean coast don't just eat *gallo pinto* (rice and beans) for breakfast, and their *casados* (set meals) have rice and beans mixed together.

Best *patis*
Taylor's Dine & Grill (p93)

Must-try *casados*
Caribbean Kalisi Coffee Shop (p93)

GETTING AROUND

Car Renting a car is the easiest way to travel El Caribe.

Public transportation Ample public transportation in Limón City, including taxis, and buses arriving from Terminal de Autobuses, and Terminal MEPE.

Taxi, shuttle and public bus Services run between Limón City, Cahuita and Puerto Viejo.

CARIBBEAN COAST FIND YOUR FEET

SEP–OCT
Dry weather means exceptional snorkeling and diving

DEC–FEB
Find epic waves in Puerto Viejo during these months

FEB–APR
Generally rainier, budget accommodations, fewer crowds

AUG–SEP
Best time to spot turtles

11 Intense
WAVES

SURFING | ADRENALINE | ADVENTURE

Consistently gnarly, advanced level Salsa Brava, aka 'The Cheese Grater,' is a wild ride, even for experienced surfers. With heavy, sizable surf and a skin-shredding coral bottom, it's Puerto Viejo's sickest break, only rivaled by Witch's Rock in intensity. While Salsa Brava attracts brave Ticos and tourists, even advanced surfers are sucked into the washing machine and smashed onto the coral below.

ADRIAN HEPWORTH/ALAMY STOCK PHOTO ©

🗺 How To

Getting here Access Salsa Brava from the very south end of Puerto Viejo on the way to Playa Cocles. Look for the small park with beach access and plenty of seasoned surfers with shortboards.

When to go You'll get awesome waves year round, but if you're really seeking a divine surf experience, visit during April or November when the swells are the biggest.

Beware! Watch out for super-sharp coral and big egos on the breaks.

LMSPENCER/SHUTTERSTOCK ©

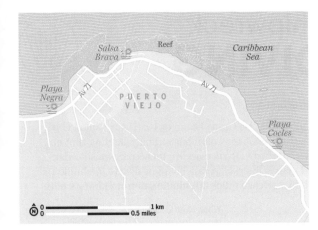

Top left Playa Cocles
Bottom left Playa Negra

🖋 Surfing Playa Cocles

A 10-minute walk or two-minute bike ride from Salsa Brava, Playa Cocles is a sweet alternative to the Cheese Grater, with intermediate to advanced waves and a less-aggressive lineup than the infamous surfer skinner.

Bring your shortboard and head to Cocles during high tide, when you'll find magnificent, hearty waves and a lengthy run. There are left and right breaks near the shore and ample room for everyone.

If your surfing skills are a little rusty and you want to warm up properly before heading to Salsa Brava, Playa Cocles is a smart play, and since it's so close, you can easily kick off both places in a day.

■ **By Alexander Tapia** of Alexander Adventures & Transfers CR, Puerto Viejo

Breaking the Pacific monopoly Puerto Viejo's Cheese Grater proves once and for all that the Península de Nicoya and the Pacific coast don't have a lockdown on fab surfing in Costa Rica. Salsa Brava not only rivals anything you'll find in Tamarindo, Jacó, or even intermediate-level Dominical, it blows it out of the water. Massive swells coupled with lacerating coral make this break a fun but ferocious ride that can give you bragging rights forever or land you in the nearest ER; no in-betweens.

Local territory Shortboards are the best way to navigate the perils and barrels of the Cheese Grater, although they won't protect you against the break's other menace: territorial surfers who stake claim to the juiciest and heaviest waves. Don't expect any courtesies or favors from salty surfers whose turf you're paddling on. If you drop in on the line, you'll get slammed with worse than Salsa Brava's notorious coral.

Takeoff zones Salsa Brava has two takeoff zones: First and Second Peak. Top surfers and locals usually flock to First Peak, and the lineup can get jammed. Second Peak tends to be less congested, and it's just a little northwest of First Peak. You can catch barrels from either takeoff point, but the Second Peak is slightly better for shoulder surfing.

Playa Negra If the Cheese Grater is too intense for your tastes, nearby Playa Negra has chiller surf and a calmer vibe.

12 Shipwreck
DIVING

DIVING | UNINHABITED | SHIPWRECK

Whether it's called Quiribri, Little Grape Island or Isla Uvita, Limón City's long and lush offshore isle was Christopher Columbus' primary landing spot on his final trip to El Caribe. It's adorned with *alemandra,* tobacco, Spanish cedar, and Peruvian Poro trees and plants. Snorkel, paddleboard or dive to the hidden shipwreck on this uninhabited stretch, a quick 30-minute sail from Limón's port.

🤿 How To

Getting here The port is a quick walk from Parque Vargas in downtown Limón City. Walk there or take a local bus. Check the ferry schedule in advance to confirm departure and return.

When to go Go during El Caribe's dry season (September to October) for the best visibility.

Lighthouse When not diving or exploring Isla Uvita's rugged landscape, pay homage to the lighthouse and its cultural significance.

SEAPHOTOART/ALAMY STOCK PHOTO ©

Surfing Massive coral reefs surround Isla Uvita and create gnarly, unpredictable, but undeniably fun surf with barrel-heavy waves and sharp breaks. Bring your shortboard if you want a challenge, but be prepared for unforgiving waves and a super-sharp coral bottom if you get stuck in the washing machine. Jellyfish are also common near Isla Uvita.

Paddleboarding and snorkeling These are other pastimes du jour off Isla Uvita, and you'll see scores of tropical fish darting around just below the surface. On-water activities are fun, and you'll get an eye-catching look at Limón from the unblemished shores of Isla Uvita.

Diving If you have the chops and desire and want to have a super-unique experience, go scuba diving. Marine life and coral have reclaimed Isla Uvita's shipwreck, the *Phoenix,* and exploring the wreck is one of the most popular and rewarding things to do here. Full of twisty nooks and glorious bright coral and sea life, the *Phoenix* is a cool interplay of sunken maritime technology and marine life habitat.

Secret getaway Isla Uvita isn't all that well known with tourists, so you'll enjoy a wholly Tico experience that seems a world away from metropolitan Limón.

Far left Snorkeling **Left** Isla Uvita from Limón City

≋ Offshore Attraction

There's an unnamed and unregulated shipwreck off the shore of Puerto Viejo. Look for the reggae beach bar beneath the Lazy Loft Hostel, and you can't miss it. Tilted on its side, graffiti-splashed and surrounded by broken glass, sharp coral, and wires, the unnamed shipwreck of Puerto Viejo is a favorite local spot to swim to and hang out.

You can swim out there, too, at your own risk. Go at lower tide, and wear proper, sturdy-soled water shoes. It's about a 10- to 15-minute swim away from the shore during good weather.

13 Sea Turtles & SECLUSION

SEA TURTLES | SPORTFISHING | BIRDWATCHING

Parismina sits at the mouth of Parque Nacional Tortuguero and is known for its leatherback sea turtles, laid-back village life, and phenomenal sportfishing and birdwatching. Visit on your way to the park, or spend a few days soaking in the local vibe, horseback riding, or fishing for bonito, snook or tarpon in the local canals or beachside.

How To

Getting here Take the public bus to Siquirries and hop on the Caño Blanco water taxi, which runs regularly, to Parismina. Or take a tour from nearby Puerto Viejo or Limón.

When to go Visit between February and July for leatherbacks, and July and October for green turtles.

Language Parismina is a local town, so you'll need some Spanish to get around.

Money No reliable ATMs in Parismina. Only a few vendors and accommodations accept credit cards; bring cash.

Map:

- 0–10 km / 0–5 miles
- Tortuguero
- Río Tortuguero
- Canales del Tortuguero
- Rogelio Pardo Jochs
- Caribbean Sea
- Parque Nacional Tortuguero
- Parismina
- Caño Blanco
- Río Parismina
- Río Reventazón
- Punta del Riel
- San Rafael
- Pier Goshen
- Río Pacuare
- Camino de Costa Rica
- Siquirres
- Batán

A different vibe Parismina's vibe is light years away from anything you'll find in Puerto Viejo or Limón City. It's a laid-back, chill, eco-centric atmosphere with tons of local homestays, plenty of traditional Costa Rican culture, and leatherback and green turtles aplenty. You won't find a party scene here. Parismina is for those who don't mind working for an exceptional experience, including taking public transportation and water taxis to land on something wholly unique. Rudimentary Spanish and a willingness to go with the flow are musts here. For the whole experience, stay with a local family.

Wildlife Situated right near Parque Nacional Tortuguero, Parismina is a veritable haven for local fish and birds, such as Agami herons, spoonbill and toucans, which, in addition to its famed turtles, flock to its beaches between February and October. You can try your luck at sportfishing right from the beach.

🚶 Walk Across Costa Rica

Pick up the **Camino de Costa Rica** – a walk that traverses Costa Rica from El Caribe to the Pacific Coast – outside Parismina at Pier Goshen. Your 174-mile walk takes just over two weeks and runs through Costa Rica's oft-overlooked internal rural villages on the way to Quepos on the Pacific Coast. You'll stay at local houses, enjoy curated activities and experiences, and support the local economy. You'll also trek through different eco-systems, including jungle and mountainous regions.

Certain parts of the trail are strenuous, so relatively high endurance and physical aptitude are required, as well as a desire to experience authentic Tico culture.

Turtles Colossal leatherback turtles arrive in the middle of February, and there are ample options to both volunteer with the turtles and observe them through local, guided nighttime tours. While it might be tempting to venture onto the beach on your own, please refrain. Guided tours help protect the leatherbacks by exposing them only to sanctioned red-tinted lights and also support the local economy.

Above Leatherback sea turtles **Left** Agami heron

14 Limón City's
FOODIES

RONDON | PATIS | TOUR

Firmly but politely hidden from outsiders and folks not in the know, Limón City's culinary scene spans a wide berth. It's evident in Jamaicatown, in Caribbean bakeries that serve sweet yucca rolls and *patis,* and in local *sodas* (small local restaurants) offering *gallo pinto* with coconut rice, as well as *rondon,* a traditional Jamaican fish stew that celebrates the African diaspora.

CENTRAL AMERICA/ALAMY STOCK PHOTO ©

🗺 **How To**

Getting around Public buses are the easiest and cheapest way to get around, but taxis are available too. Always use the meter.

Tips Check out the Mercado Municipal for goodies and cashew wine, the open-air market near Parque Vargas for the best organic fruits and vegetables, and visit Jamaicatown. *Sodas* are scattered throughout the city, serving riffs on traditional *casados* with coconut milk. Garlic potatoes, *patis* and Caribbean sweets are abundant.

CONTENT ZILLA/SHUTTERSTOCK ©

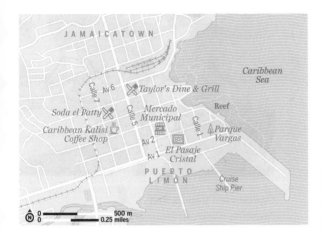

Culinary heritage Part of Limón City's charm is tied to its culinary heritage. Food is intrinsically linked to the culture here, and it has deep roots dating back to when seeds were taken from Jamaica to grow in El Caribe. The fusion of traditional Costa Rican foods with Caribbean-inspired ingredients is one of Limón City's critical contributions to the foodie world, including coconut-milk-flavored rice and beans instead of more standard *gallo pinto*.

Visit Limón City's **open-air market** near Parque Vargas for fresh, inexpensive organic fruits; Jamaicatown for famous fried chicken; and any number of small Caribbean Bakeries for sharp ginger biscuits or yucca rolls. *Rondon,* sometimes spelled 'run down' or 'run dun,' is a traditional Jamaican stew with a coconut-milk base, plantains, yams, onions, tomatoes, and a variety of different shellfish or local seafood, like red snapper. Served alongside bread or rice, it's a delightful dish.

Food tours and eateries Take a traditional food tour out of Limón City itself, or visit **Soda el Patty** or **Caribbean Kalisi Coffee Shop** for a memorable meal. **Taylor's Dine & Grill**, a fantastic spot for spicy *pati* (savory pastries), sits right across the street from the former location of the old Black Star Line building, a relic of Marcus Garvey's legacy on the Caribbean coast. **Soul Life Tours** offers fantastic and comprehensive Limón City food tours that combine history with the area's culinary scene.

Top left Open-air market, Limón City
Bottom left Jerk chicken

🖼 Limón City's Underground Art Scene

Sharp-eyed visitors will spot street art near Parque Vargas on Limón City's dock, right across from Isla Uvita, where Christopher Columbus famously made his fourth and final voyage to Costa Rica. There are also many smaller museums near Parque Vargas, directly across from where the cruise ships dock, showcasing historical oil paintings. If you're looking for super local, new art, visit **El Pasaje Cristal**, reasonably close to Parque Vargas, where local artists set up shop. It's across the street from Pops ice cream shop, right near Banco Nacional, two blocks from the park near Calle 2.

■ By Sadie Jordan, *Soul Life Travel*
ⓘ *Soullifetravel*

Unpacking Limón City

FABULOUS FOOD, ESSENTIAL HISTORY AND WELCOMING VIBES

Limón City is among the most important historic areas in Costa Rica, thanks to Marcus Garvey's Black Star Line and his UNIA organization. From its tantalizing Caribbean takes on traditional Costa Rican foods to its essential history, Limón City beckons you toward a whole new appreciation of Costa Rica.

Top left Marcus Garvey **Top center** United Fruit Company workers **Top right** Stock certificate, Black Star Line

Undeserved Reputation

Despite its incredible historical relevance and food scene, many visitors to Costa Rica give Limón City a miss, as the town has been unfairly maligned as a risky no-go zone. That's a shame because, while parts of the city are best avoided, and you should always exercise caution with your valuables, it's no worse or better than other major tourist cities in Costa Rica.

Jamaican Immigration

Limón City, and El Caribe in general, have a predominately Black population due to the influx of Jamaican migrants and the United Fruit Company's history in Limón City. Jamaican people emigrated to Costa Rica during the mid-1800s to work on the new railroad and for the United Fruit Company. They brought their cuisine with them, and the merging of Jamaican staples like jerk chicken and meats with Costa Rican dishes created the amazing food culture El Caribe enjoys today.

Marcus Garvey

What Marcus Garvey did for both the people of Limón City and Puerto Viejo, and African American people in general, should be promoted and celebrated. Garvey's Black Star Line had the objective of facilitating trade and giving Black people the agency to travel back to Africa if they wished. His Universal Negro Improvement Association, or UNIA, had members worldwide.

Like many other Jamaican-born people, Garvey emigrated to Costa Rica for job prospects and found himself

working at United Fruit Company. There, Garvey witnessed exploitation and terrible working conditions, prompting him to launch *The Nation*, a publication aimed at unmasking cruel conditions and supporting workers. Garvey's activism at the United Fruit Company led him to become a staunch advocate for Black people, found the UNIA and the Black Star Line, and facilitate the development of community centers in El Caribe.

> Limón City's charm comes from its historic significance, a legacy of overcoming the odds, friendly, proud people, and remarkable food and arts scenes.

You can see Garvey's legacy all over Limón City and see the fruits of his labor continued in places like Puerto Viejo, where Garvey set up a haven house for migrant workers who didn't have anywhere else to go. Today, it's a thriving community center.

Limón City Today

Despite being long overlooked in favor of the Pacific coast, weathering decades of economic recession, and taking a huge hit from the cruise-ship industry, Limón City retains its dignity and culture. The city's charm comes from its historic significance; a legacy of overcoming the odds; friendly, proud people; and remarkable food and arts scenes.

So, don't believe the hype about Limón City. Instead have a *pati*, a yucca roll, or a steaming bowl of *rondon,* visit the old site of the Black Star Line, learn about Garvey's profound legacy, and walk away with an appreciation for the grit and dignity of El Caribe's people.

ⓘ **United Fruit Company**

While the American-owned United Fruit Company, known as Chiquita today, promised jobs and mobility to Limón City's residents, the reality was sadly much different. Workers were paid abysmal wages, sometimes in company coupons rather than actual cash, and expected to work long hours with no time off. Additionally, vast banana plantations destabilized the natural environment and negatively affected the soil, impacting future generations. Workers often suffered through bouts of tropical diseases, like yellow fever or even malaria, and sanitary conditions were poor at best. At its peak, the United Fruit Company owned as much as 9% of Costa Rica's land.

15 Community **HEART**

HISTORY | COMMUNITY | ART

The Yellow House, as it's locally known, is the epicenter of Puerto Viejo's community. A free space for the people, gifted to the people by Marcus Garvey, it embodies multiple forms, from a thriving cultural center and historical site to an artistic hub. It's a piece of 'real Puerto Viejo,' speaking to the town's history and its ongoing commitment to its people.

🗺 How To

Getting here Casa de la Cultura is about two blocks from Chino Beach on Calle 215. If you hit the 256, you've gone too far. It's also a few blocks away from Puerto Viejo's central bus station, so if you're coming in from San José, walk along Chino Beach away from Puerto Viejo's main beach and hang a right on Calle 215.

Do your research Check the Facebook page of Casa de la Cultura in advance to see what's happening before you visit.

Caribbean Sea

Reef

El Barco Hundido

Salsa Brava

Casa de la Cultura

Soda Tamara

PUERTO VIEJO

Av. 73

Av. 71

Calle 215

Av. 67

Playa Negra

Calle 213

Soccer Field

0 — 500 m
0 — 0.25 miles

The Yellow House Puerto Viejo's **Casa de la Cultura**, or House of Culture, also known as Liberty Hall and the 'Yellow House,' is right across from Cafe Viejo and is an essential piece of Puerto Viejo's history and Marcus Garvey's legacy. Made for and given to the people by

Garvey, the humble yellow house was a place where migrant workers could come if they didn't have a place to live. It was and continues to be a community hub and a marketplace. With murals inside and out depicting its history, and a banner honoring the first families

of Puerto Viejo, the house holds a regular flea market and ongoing events. Since its inception, its importance as a community asset have only increased. Although the schedule has changed somewhat due to COVID restrictions, it still hosts health fairs, English classes, dance

🚢 The Black Star Line

Before it burned down, Liberty Hall in Limón City housed Marcus Garvey's Black Star Line, an integral part of Garvey's 'Back to Africa Movement.' The Black Star Line transported goods throughout the African diaspora and gave African Americans the option of returning to Africa. An activist and the founder of the Universal Negro Improvement Association and African Communities League (UNIA-ACL), Jamaican-born Garvey and his Black Star Line and UNIA-ACL are widely credited with empowering formerly enslaved people in Costa Rica, which is why he's honored today.

Even though Limón City's Liberty Hall is no longer in existence, it remains a symbol of Garvey's legacy and commitment to Afro Costa Ricans.

and documentary screenings. It also offers an on-site library, regular art exhibitions, children's entertainment and education, and student-led workshops too. Since it's not open all of the time, and activities are restricted due to COVID, check its Facebook page for a calendar of ongoing events and more information.

Refueling Make sure you grab a quick bite to eat at nearby **Tamara's** before or after visiting Marcus Garvey's yellow house. Tamara's is a Black-owned, family restaurant where you can dine on typical El Caribe fare, learn more about Garvey's legacy and read some of his most famous quotes on the walls.

Above Casa de la Cultura

16 Waterfalls & **POOLS**

WATERFALLS | CALYPSO | WILDLIFE

Cahuita has a unique vibe, played to the tune of Calypso music from centenarian local legend Walter 'Gavitt' Ferguson. Explore private, earthquake-forged pools and clandestine waterfalls, meet the Bribrí indigenous people, and experience an authentic, unforgettable slice of Afro-Caribbean paradise.

How To

Getting here Cahuita is a short, straight-shot, 50-minute bus ride down the coast from Limón, or 30-minutes from Puerto Viejo in the opposite direction. Since it's only a handful of streets, walking is the easiest way to get around, although you can always rent a bike to explore Cahuita in a flash, or check out the surrounding countryside.

When to go Visit between June and September to glimpse leatherback turtles nesting on Cahuita's *playas*.

Walter 'Gavitt' Ferguson

Also known as 'Segundo,' Ferguson is easily Cahuita's most famous resident and the king of Calypso in this chilled-out, lovely Caribbean town. Those seeking an alternative to the reggae beats of Puerto Viejo will find Cahuita's weekly music scene refreshing, and if you're lucky, you might even get to meet the legendary Mr Gavitt yourself.

Low Key & Friendly

Cahuita's charms fly under the tourist radar, so experiences such as visiting waterfalls or seeing leatherbacks are likely to be intimate and memorable, and to directly benefit the local community.

In Cahuita, in-the-know travelers will seek out secluded **natural swimming pools**, formed in 1991 after a large earthquake created a barrier between the sea and Cahuita's

(i) Yellow Eyelash Vipers

A strike from a yellow eyelash viper lands a heavy dose of venom that immediately attacks the nervous system. Death is quick but terrifying, making these brightly hued snakes one of the most fearsome creatures in Central America. Fortunately, if you give them a wide berth, you'll avoid their wrath.

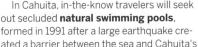

Top left Cahuita beach **Top right** Natureal swimming pool, Cahuita **Bottom left** Playa Negra (p100)

beaches. Other attractions include **Playa Negra**, a fabulous and relaxed black-sand beach, and Cahuita's petite and peaceful **waterfalls** with natural pools, a local haunt where you might mingle with Ticos or possibly nobody at all.

Leatherback Turtles

Cahuita Turtle Rescue nurtures and protects resident leatherback turtles that nest on the beach between June and September.

Visit during those months and watch these beautiful behemoths emerge from the sea and lay their eggs. Since sea turtles are easily spooked, hiring a local guide and avoiding flash photography is the most ethical and best way to see them.

Parque Nacional Cahuita

While Cahuita isn't on a lot of travelers' radars, Parque Nacional Cahuita is undeniably touristy. It's famous for a reason: it's packed

ⓘ Visiting the Bribrí People

The indigenous Bribrí people live 20 minutes outside Cahuita. Although it's not advisable or respectful to go alone, local guides from Cahuita can take you to the village, where you'll learn how to make chocolate, fashion a rope of local leaves and learn about Bribrí farming techniques. There are also three incredible waterfalls near the Bribrí village and a lookout point from which you can spot the Cordillera de Talamanca mountains, Panama and Puerto Viejo. Visiting the Bribrí people is an honor and a privilege. If you go, refrain from photographing them or their homes without permission.

■ By Alexander Mullins Aymerich (Tito Cahuita), *owner of Cahuita Green Tours, Cahuita*
🔘 *tito_cahuita*

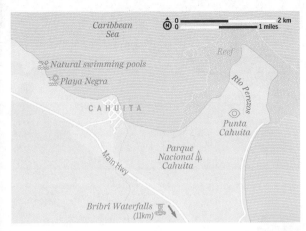

Left Sloth, Parque Nacional Cahuita
Below Yellow eyelash vipers, Parque Nacional Cahuita

with all manner of animal life, such as capuchin monkeys, bats, howler monkeys, raccoons and sloths. The best place to see these animals is about three-quarters of a mile down the trail toward the park's second river. Keep your eyes on the trees for the elusive toucans that call the national park home.

Parque Nacional Cahuita is one of the premier spots in the country to see yellow eyelash vipers. These vivid, lemon-colored snakes are super-venomous, but not as aggressive as Costa Rica's deadly fer-du-lance. Photograph them from a distance and without a flash to avoid spooking the shy creatures.

An incredible place to swim because the water is always balmy and calm, **Punta Cahuita** is ringed with white-sand beaches and full of tropical fish like loro, angelfish, red snapper, kingfish and friendly nurse sharks. Snorkeling is best during the dry season, as Costa Rica's green season can stir up sediment from the bottom and disturb the fish. However, swimming is fine all year round, as there are no rips or significant currents near Punta Cahuita.

Guided and solo tours of national parks are available, although you'll probably spot more animals, like hidden howler monkeys and two-toed sloths, if you go with a guide.

17

Rainforest
RELAXING

REEFS | RAINFORST | REFUGE

Manzanillo is an oft-overlooked fishing village in the Gandoca–Manzanillo Wildlife Refuge near the Panama border, with scores of protected reefs, white-sand beaches and gentle leatherback turtles. Shrouded in rainforest and low-key, Manzanillo is a bright-and-early alternative to Puerto Viejo's raucous nighttime party scene.

📷 How To

Getting here/around
Manzanillo is 14km south of Puerto Viejo, near the Panamanian border. Arrive by bus from San José or Puerto Viejo, or hop on a shuttle bound for the border. Once here, you'll only need your feet to get around.

When to go September to October for snorkeling, July to September for turtle-watching

Practicalities You'll need some Spanish, as many locals aren't bilingual. There aren't reliable ATMs, so stock up on colones in Puerto Viejo.

Village Life

A quarter of a century old, and full of quaint curving streets and brightly colored stilted buildings, **Manzanillo** is a charming coastal village. If you're looking for a break from Puerto Viejo's party scene and want some peak *pura vida*, this place is the place for it.

Manzanillo isn't the southernmost stop on the way out of Costa Rica (that honor belongs to Sixaola), but it's only a few miles shy of the border. So if you want to tick off Panama's Caribbean coast and El Caribe in one go, it's a smart, time-sensitive choice because you can be in Panama's Bocas del Toro in a matter of hours.

Although Manzanillo gets tourists – especially during turtle season when you can take guided tours of leatherback nesting sites – it doesn't specifically cater to them in the way larger,

☆ Under the Sea

A plethora of animals lives off Manzanillo's reef-fringed shores. Dip under the waves to check out parrotfish (loro), shrimp, angelfish, lobsters, sea stars, manatees and dolphins. Sea urchins, sponges and anemones are common too. You'll find all manner of crabs and pelicans near the beach, plus bright toucans in the trees.

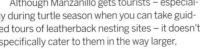

Top left Manzanillo **Top right** Comet sea star, sea sponge and anemone
Bottom left Capuchin monkey

more popular towns do. As such, it's a good idea to have at least a rudimentary understanding of Spanish and not expect many food options or upscale accommodations. Many of the roads are rough, there aren't serviceable ATMs, and the nearest large pharmacies and hospitals are in Puerto Viejo.

Turtles Galore

Narrow walking paths, bright azure waters and stretches of white sand protected as part of the **Gandoca-Manzanillo Wildlife Refuge** are the prime draws here. Plus, you can stay in humble accommodations and homestays, wake up to sea birds and chattering monkeys every morning, and see leatherback turtles nesting between February and September. If you want to see tiny leatherbacks taking their first steps toward the sea, visit between April and May. Occasionally green and hawksbill turtles grace Manzanillo's shores too.

🔭 When the Beach is Bathed in Red

Manzanillo is a fantastic, less-touristed spot to see huge leatherbacks, hawksbills and green turtles, but you won't catch them in the brilliant light of a thousand flashes. White lights spook turtles, sending them plodding back into the sea. So instead, during nesting season, guides use ruby-colored flashlights to gently illuminate the creatures, allowing the turtles to do their business and educating visitors simultaneously.

If you visit the turtles, it's essential to check your phone beforehand to make sure the flash is off. Even one bright light can prompt a mama leatherback to abandon her nesting and disturb the laying process.

Far Left Sea turtle **Left** Gandoca-Manzanillo Wildlife Refuge **Below** Green iguana

Snorkeling & Swimming

Manzanillo's reefs provide plenty of snorkeling opportunities. You may spot tropical loros, angel-fish and nurse sharks in these waters. If you're extra fortunate, you might even come across a manatee. Sea kayaking and swimming are also popular activities. Manzanillo's calm waters are good for swimming year round, but dry-season snorkeling when there's less loose sediment and better visibility tends to be better.

Humans & Animals Side-by-Side

Firmly rooted in traditional Costa Rican life, Manzanilla is rustic and unapologetically itself. The town goes to bed and wakes up early. Manzanillo's human residents live side by side with giant iguanas, sloths and howler monkeys. Capuchins, tapirs and pacas also reside nearby. The rainforest climate and underdeveloped beauty of Manzanillo make it an apex place for jungle bugs, scorpions and sometimes snakes.

These rugged brushes with the animal kingdom are all part of Manzanillo's charm. It's the textbook definition of the overused and often poorly applied term 'off the beaten path' and an unconventional place to lay your head in El Caribe.

18
Unplugged & IMMERSED

NATURE | WILDLIFE | MARINE ACTIVITIES

▬▬▬ Step outside Limón City and Puerto Viejo, and you'll find swatches of rainforest, hidden waterfalls, secret beach pools and carefree rural life just a few miles from the Panama border. Leave the amenities of home and the hassle of instant communication behind.

DAMSEA/SHUTTERSTOCK ©

🗺 Trip Notes

Getting here/around Start either in Manzanillo or Parismina. Travel between Manzanillo and Cahuita by shuttle or bus going toward Puerto Viejo. Hop aboard a water taxi to reach Parismina.

When to go Go during August and September for the best snorkeling conditions and turtle spotting. Plus, prices tend to dip during the late summer months, so you'll hit the sweet spot of great weather and affordable accommodations.

Amenities Don't expect solid wi-fi or lots of amenities in these towns.

🦶 Natural Getaway

It's all about nature and chill. Enjoy amazing snorkeling and up-close animal sightings in Manzanillo (pictured above), then head up to Cahuita's pristine Playa Negra and jungle waterfalls. Parismina has some of the best sportfishing and nature in the country, locked away from the land by the sea and several rivers.

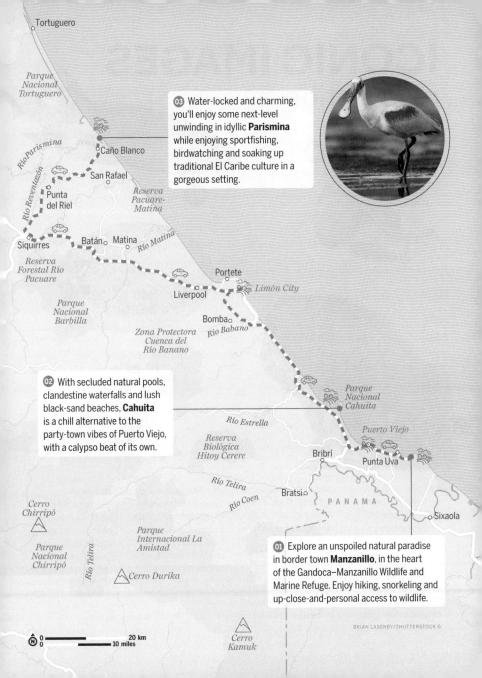

Tortuguero

Parque Nacional Tortuguero

Río Parismina

Caño Blanco

San Rafael

Río Reventazón

Punta del Riel

Siquirres

Batán

Matina

Río Matina

Reserva Pacuare-Matina

Reserva Forestal Río Pacuare

Parque Nacional Barbilla

Zona Protectora Cuenca del Río Banano

Portete

Liverpool

Limón City

Bomba

Río Babano

Parque Nacional Cahuita

Río Estrella

Reserva Biológica Hitoy Cerere

Puerto Viejo

Bribrí

Punta Uva

Río Telira

Río Coen

Bratsi

PANAMA

Sixaola

Cerro Chirripó

Parque Nacional Chirripó

Río Telira

Parque Internacional La Amistad

Cerro Durika

03 Water-locked and charming, you'll enjoy some next-level unwinding in idyllic **Parismina** while enjoying sportfishing, birdwatching and soaking up traditional El Caribe culture in a gorgeous setting.

02 With secluded natural pools, clandestine waterfalls and lush black-sand beaches, **Cahuita** is a chill alternative to the party-town vibes of Puerto Viejo, with a calypso beat of its own.

01 Explore an unspoiled natural paradise in border town **Manzanillo**, in the heart of the Gandoca–Manzanillo Wildlife and Marine Refuge. Enjoy hiking, snorkeling and up-close-and-personal access to wildlife.

BRIAN LASENBY/SHUTTERSTOCK ©

N 0 ———— 20 km
   0 ———— 10 miles

Cerro Kamuk

ICONIC IMAGES
of El Caribe

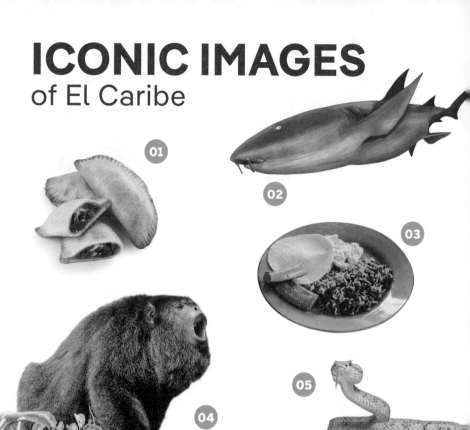

01

02

03

05

04

01 Pati
A delicious El Caribe spin on *empanadas* containing savory, traditional Costa Rican fillings, and a tasty specialty in Limón City.

02 Nurse shark
Snorkel Parque Nacional Cahuita, and you could have a chance encounter with these majestic ancient and completely non-aggressive creatures.

03 Fusion cuisine
Coconut-scented rice and hearty meats offer a spin on *gallo pinto*, a terrific nod to Jamaican influence in El Caribe.

04 Howler monkey
Some of Manzanillo's loudest but most lovable residents, these small black monkeys make a racket disproportionate to their diminutive size.

05 Yellow eyelash viper
One of the most venomous snakes in Cahuita, eyelash vipers are shy, vibrant, and amazing creatures indigenous to El Caribe.

06 Shortboard
Ideal for making sharp turns on Salsa Brava's 'Cheese Grater', shortboards allow you to slice through tough waves with ease.

07 Playa Negra
Cahuita's Playa Negra (p100), a black-sand beach, is an otherworldly place to spend your day and is symbolic of the town's natural beauty.

08 Black Star Line logo
Marcus Garvey's famous transportation line designed to connect to the African diaspora and transport goods and people around the world.

09 Red hummingbird
Costa Rica's Camino de Costa Rica, which starts in Parismina and continues to the Pacific, is marked with red hummingbirds.

10 Marcus Garvey
Limón City's influential activist, orator, and Black Star Line and UNIA founder (p94) who advocated tirelessly to unite the African diaspora.

Listings

BEST OF THE REST

Best Eats in El Caribe

Taylor's Dine & Grill $$

A great spot for authentic *patis* and coconut rice and beans, situated across the street from the former location of Marcus Garvey's Black Star Line.

Mercado Municipal $

Visit this large market right near Limón City's port for authentic souvenirs and great local food at a fraction of the price you would pay elsewhere.

Soda El Patty $

Enjoy *patis* and live music at this affordable Limón City *soda*. It's got a welcoming vibe and fun atmosphere that will make you feel right at home.

Bar Tsunami $$$

Nice spot for fresh sushi rolls and a party vibe. Prices are higher than local *sodas,* but are still reasonable enough for budget travelers.

Caribbean Kalisi Coffee Shop $$

An ideal brunch spot. Visit for some of the best and strongest coffee in El Caribe and generously portioned plates of traditional Caribbean Costa Rican fare.

Shugaa Place $$

Slightly more expensive than your typical local *soda,* but has great ambience and really good artisanal coffees. It's a nice place to chill and get your bearings while in Limón City.

Cafe Rico $

Puerto Viejo's top spot for fast, delicious breakfasts and traditional *soda* fare.

Staying in Puerto Viejo

Selina Puerto Viejo

Slightly down from the main beach and rasta bars, Selina has upscale hostel vibes, with both shared and private accommodations and an on-site pool.

Villas Pina

Adults-only resort close to Puerto Viejo and Playa Negra, with a sizable pool, plenty of hammocks, amenities, and a relaxed and secluded location.

Rockin J's Hostel

In the middle of Puerto Viejo, this hostel has a party vibe, huge grounds and strong wi-fi. There are only private rooms, so if you need a dorm, go elsewhere.

Jaguar Inn Bungalows

Set back slightly into the jungle, this secluded natural hotel has plenty of gardens and decent wi-fi. It's a good respite from the beach parties of Puerto Viejo.

Traditional *soda*, Puerto Viejo

El Caribe Best Nightlife

Coco's Bar y Restaurante $$

Cahuita rasta bar with calypso and reggae music, a great menu and plenty of regular drink specials.

Splash $$$

An upper-scale sushi and wine bar with live music right in the middle of Cahuita's principal road. It gets busy on weekends.

Reggae Bar $

Decent Cahuita spot for food. Great place for drinks and socializing very close to Playa Negra.

Ricky's Place $

Solid spot for big portions of fresh seafood and a wide selection of different drinks and beers. In Cahuita.

Cahuita Taste Cider and Shine $$$

Artisanal ciders featuring local flavors in an upscale brewery environment fairly close to the city.

Maestro's Wine & Grill $$$

Limón City's premier wine and craft-beer bar, with tasty tapas and a nice vibe.

Tasty Waves Cantina $$

Chilled-out Puerto Viejo haunt with excellent food, occasional live music and a friendly atmosphere.

 Top Tour Companies in El Caribe

Soul Life Travel

Located in Puerto Viejo but running tours in Limón City and Puerto Viejo, Soul Life Travel works with the community providing local experiences that put money in local people's pockets.

Caribe Fun Tours

Offering a variety of cultural and adventure-oriented experiences, Caribe Fun Tours will

Salsa Brava

help you understand and appreciate El Caribe on a whole new level. It's based in Puerto Viejo, but serves all of El Caribe.

Cahuita Green Tours

Locally owned and operated, in El Caribe's town of Cahuita, Cahuita Green Tours specializes in taking tourists to hidden waterfalls and beaches, and meeting the Bribrí people in a respectful and educational fashion.

Bars with a View in Puerto Viejo

Salsa Brava $$

Named for the famous surf spot, Salsa Brava offers incredible views of the break and drink specials to go along with it.

Lazy Mon $

You'll get regular music, cheap drinks and a view of Puerto Viejo's shipwreck at this super-popular beach bar.

Johnny's Place $

Whether you're watching the surf or checking out the game on the bar's large TV, Johnny's Place is a humble spot at which to soak up the sun with a cold one.

 Scan to find more things to do in the Caribbean Coast online

NORTHERN
COSTA RICA

WILDLIFE | VOLCANOES | FARMS

**Experience
Northern
Costa Rica
online**

Witness the power of the highly active **Volcán Rincón de la Vieja** (p140)
🚗 40mins from Liberia

Lounge on deserted beaches and swim in the serene **Golfo de Santa Elena** (p148)
🚗 1hr from Liberia

Swim under a waterfall at **Llanos de Cortés** (p139)
🚗 30mins from Liberia

Swim in the dreamy blue waters of the **Río Celeste** (p144)
🚗 30mins from Bijagua

Golfo de Santa Elena

La Cruz
Puerto Doley
El Jobo
Cuajiniquil

Parque Nacional Guanacaste Volcán Cacao

Quebrada Grande

Volcán Rincón de la Vieja

Parque Nacional Rincón de la Vieja

Rinconcito

Curubandé

Guayabo

Fortuna de Bagaces

Volcán Miravalles

Río Pizote

Upala

Aguas Claras Canalete

Bijagua *Río Celeste*

Volcán Tenorio

Parque Nacional Volcán Tenorio

Lago Cote

Tilarán

Pijije *Río Piedras* Bagaces

Río Tenorio

Corobicí

Isla Chira

Golfo de Nicoya

NORTHERN COSTA RICA
Trip Builder

A microcosm of Costa Rica itself, this diverse region shows off the country's highlights, from the steaming volcanoes and misty cloud forests of the Cordillera de Guanacaste, to the inky lagoons and dense rainforest of the Northern Lowlands.

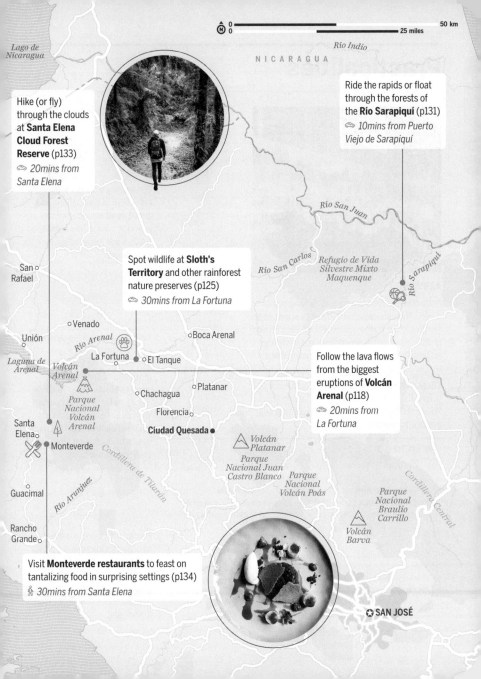

NICARAGUA

Lago de Nicaragua

Río Indio

Río San Juan

Hike (or fly) through the clouds at **Santa Elena Cloud Forest Reserve** (p133)
🚗 *20mins from Santa Elena*

Ride the rapids or float through the forests of the **Río Sarapiquí** (p131)
🚗 *10mins from Puerto Viejo de Sarapiquí*

Spot wildlife at **Sloth's Territory** and other rainforest nature preserves (p125)
🚗 *30mins from La Fortuna*

Río San Carlos

Refugio de Vida Silvestre Mixto Maquenque

Río Sarapiquí

San Rafael ○

○ Venado

○ Boca Arenal

Unión ○

Río Arenal

La Fortuna 🐾 ○

○ El Tanque

Laguna de Arenal

Volcán Arenal

○ Chachagua

○ Platanar

Parque Nacional Volcán Arenal

Florencia ○

Ciudad Quesada ●

Follow the lava flows from the biggest eruptions of **Volcán Arenal** (p118)
🚗 *20mins from La Fortuna*

Santa Elena ○

Monteverde

Cordillera de Tilarán

△ *Volcán Platanar*

Parque Nacional Juan Castro Blanco

Parque Nacional Volcán Poás

Cordillera Central

Guacimal ○

Río Aranjuez

Parque Nacional Braulio Carrillo

Rancho Grande ○

△ *Volcán Barva*

Visit **Monteverde restaurants** to feast on tantalizing food in surprising settings (p134)
🚶 *30mins from Santa Elena*

✪ **SAN JOSÉ**

Practicalities

ARRIVING

Daniel Oduber Quirós International Airport, Liberia This smal airport provides easy access to destinations in the northern parts of Costa Rica. Private shuttles run from the airport to various destinations, and public buses run from the terminal in Liberia.

Juan Santamaría International Airport, San José The main international airport is closer to destinations in the northeast, including the Sarapiquí region. Private shuttles run from airport, and public buses from the terminals in San José.

WHEN TO GO

JAN–APR
Peak tourist season sees the driest weather and highest prices

MAY–AUG
'Green' season brings more rain and slightly lower prices

SEP–OCT
Low season, with the most rain and lowest prices

NOV–DEC
Rain eases and the tourists return in droves during holiday season

HOW MUCH FOR A

Casado (set meal)
US$5–8

250g bag of coffee beans
US$5–8

Birding tour
US$60

GETTING AROUND

Car Renting a car gives the greatest access to destinations and activities all around the northern region. It's worth upgrading to a 4WD vehicle, especially during the rainy season.

Shuttle service A few different private shuttle services provide transportation to the main tourist destinations, including both airports, Monteverde (Santa Elena), La Fortuna and Puerto Viejo de Sarapiquí. These vans are significantly faster and more comfortable (though more expensive) than public buses.

Public bus Liberia is a major transportation center for buses traveling the Interamericana, from Santa Cruz to San José. Ciudad Quesada (San Carlos) is a transportation hub for the region further east.

EATING & DRINKING

In Guanacaste, the staple ingredient is corn, featured in corn tortillas, corn rice and especially *chorreadas* (corn pancakes; pictured top right). This is also cattle country, so this is the place to feast on grilled steaks (pictured bottom right) and burgers. Further east, the landscape is dominated by agriculture, especially plantations growing banana, pineapple and palmitos. This region is big on farm-to-table cooking, so you'll see all of these items on menus.

Best coffee
Café Monteverde
(p155)

Must-try *chorreadas*
La Choza del Maíz
(p154)

NORTHERN COSTA RICA FIND YOUR FEET

WHERE TO STAY

Depending on the length of your trip, you may want to stay in a few different towns or villages to sample this diverse region.

CONNECT & FIND YOUR WAY

Wi-fi Wi-fi is available at most lodges, hotels and restaurants, though the speed varies. Some places to stay may offer wi-fi only in common areas, not in the rooms.

Navigation Car-rental companies no longer offer GPS units, but navigation apps like Google Drive and Waze are reliably accurate.

Town/Village	Pro/Con
La Fortuna	Many options for volcano and rainforest activities. Lodging at all price points.
Monteverde/Santa Elena	Premiere cloud forest destination. Many options for activities and lodging.
Liberia	Transportation hub. Decent lodging and restaurants. Beaches and volcanoes within day-trip range.
Sarapiquí	Off-the-beaten-track destination with rainforests and rafting. Good stop-off to/from Caribbean coast.
Bijagua	Lesser-known destination offering wildlife, hiking and adventure. Good stop-off to/from Pacific coast.
Curubandé	Excellent base for volcano and adventure activities. Limited lodging and dining.

STAY IN THE LOOP

La Voz de Guanacaste (vozdeguanacaste.com) A great source for news and articles about current events, culture, the environment and human-rights issues

MONEY

Credit cards are widely accepted, but some lodgings and tour companies accept cash payment only (Costa Rican colones or US dollars). ATMs – accessible in most towns – may dispense dollars and/or colones.

19

Hot Springs &
VOLCANOES

GEOLOGY | HIKING | SOAKING

There's something awestriking about being in the shadow of an active volcano – seeing wisps of smoke drift from its conical top, following trails of volcanic rock and soaking in waters heated by volcanic thermal energy. Volcán Arenal may no longer be spitting fire, but its power is still on full display.

🗺 How To

Getting here/around
This experience requires a vehicle, although any tour agency in La Fortuna can arrange transportation to the volcano parks or to the hot springs.

When to go It's best to hike in the morning to avoid the afternoon heat. (Volcano hikes are not as shady as forest hikes.) Thermal springs are open for daytime admission (9am to 4pm) or evening admission (4pm to 9pm).

How much Admission to the national park is US$15. Eco Termales is US$44.

Hike the Lava Flows

The mighty **Volcán Arenal** is surrounded by protected land in the form of the eponymous national park, as well as private reserves, which offer chances to explore the volcano and witness its effects. The **Parque Nacional Volcán Arenal** (Sector Volcan) is the natural starting point. Arrive early to beat the heat (and maybe some of the crowds), and drive directly to the second parking lot for easiest access to the trails.

There are basically two interconnected circular trails. The **Sendero Las Coladas** (Lava Flow Traill) branches around the volcano for 2km, passing the lava field that remains from an eruption in 1992. You can actually hike up the old lava flow – now hardened into volcanic rocks – which culminates at a vista of Arenal in all its glory. A challenging but rewarding detour!

🍴 Lunch with a View

After working up an appetite on the trails, it's time to break for lunch at **Que Rico**, 12km east of the national park. Floor-to-ceiling glass walls mean that every table has an amazing view of Volcán Arenal.

Top left Volcán Arenal **Top right** Arenal 1968 trail (p120) **Bottom left** Warning signs, Parque Nacional Volcán Arenal

The 3km **Sendero El Ceibo** is a semicircular loop that branches off from Las Coladas and heads deeper into the rainforest. You might see some wildlife on this portion of the hike, but the highlight is the massive 400-year-old ceibo tree.

Circle back to the parking lot and end your hike at the **Mirador Principal**, or main lookout point, which is the closest you can get to the volcano.

Note that **Arenal 1968** is a private reserve right next the national park that offers a very similar hiking experience on and around the lava flows from the 1968 eruption. The entrance fee is slightly higher, but it's a solid alternative to the national park.

Get a Ride

If hiking doesn't get your heart pumping, there are other ways to explore the unique, post-eruption environment around Volcán Arenal.

ⓘ Local Soak

Tourists flock to the hot springs facilities around town, but locals know where to soak for free. Opposite the entrance to Tabacón Hot Springs (7km east of the national park), a gravel path leads down to **Río Chollin**, a bubbling, volcano-heated, thermal river, carefully crafted by Mother Nature. It is less luxurious and less safe than the private hot springs around town, but it's also less expensive (aka free). Be careful of strong currents and slippery rocks: water shoes are recommended. But if you're up for a mini-adventure, this is a fun, low-investment and decidedly authentic experience for travelers in the know. Enjoy!

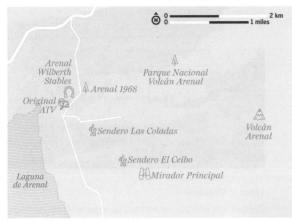

Arenal Wilberth Stables

Parque Nacional Volcán Arenal

Original ATV

Arenal 1968

Sendero Las Coladas

Volcán Arenal

Sendero El Ceibo

Mirador Principal

Laguna de Arenal

Left Thermal springs, Parque Nacional Volcán Arenal **Below** Eco Termales Fortuna

▶ Go mountain biking with **Bike Arenal** at **Arenal 1968**, where the 16km of single and double-track trails are separate from the lava hiking trails.

▶ Take a wild ride with **Original ATV** on a private farm near the national park, with volcano views all around. Along the way, you can cool off (and clean off) with a dip in the river.

▶ Ride a horse from **Arenal Wilberth Stables** through forest and farmland, near the base of the volcano. Enjoy lake and volcano views from the saddle.

Hot Stuff

After a day of hiking (or riding), you deserve to soothe your aching bones. From the park, drive 14km east to **Eco Termales Fortuna** to soak in volcano-heated waters amid verdant secondary forest. Although Eco Termales is not the fanciest 'hot springs' experience in La Fortuna, it does benefit from a gorgeous natural setting, with lush greenery all around. The large, manmade thermal pools range in temperature from 32°C to 40°C (90°F to 104°F). You can stand under a waterfall for hydromassage, and bring your body temperature down in cool water pools. Order a cocktail from the bar and sink into the warm healing waters of Mother Earth.

Volcano Power

HARNESSING GEOTHERMAL ENERGY TO SAVE THE PLANET

Since 2015, Costa Rica has generated more than 98% of its electric energy from renewable resources – one of only four countries in the world to do so. While most of this energy comes from hydropower, some 15% is geothermal power – that is, the power of the earth itself.

JOSHUA TEN BRINK/SHUTTERSTOCK ©

How it Works

Geothermal energy comes from deep beneath the surface of the earth, where a continual process of radioactive decay generates intense heat. These extreme temperatures create the semi-molten material at the earth's core known as magma. This energy is visible to us at the surface in places where cracks or fissures allow the heat to escape, such as geysers, fumaroles and hot springs. Sometimes the magma itself bubbles to the surface and flows out as lava, in a volcanic eruption.

To generate electricity, geothermal plants tap into reservoirs of hot water several kilometers beneath the surface. The hot liquid is pumped up to the surface and into a depressurizing system. The resulting steam powers a turbine, which connects to a generator to produce electricity. This 'flash-steam' system is the most common type of geothermal power plant.

Geothermal energy is a renewable resource. It is relatively clean, producing little waste or byproduct. It is also not dependent on the weather, unlike solar, wind and hydro power. It is – arguably – the ultimate 'green' energy.

Where it Works

Costa Rica is perfectly placed to tap into this practically unlimited source of energy (as evidenced by its many volcanoes). The country's first facility was the Miravalles geothermal power plant, constructed in 1994 in Bagaces. Volcán Miravalles is officially dormant, but it still generates an abundance of geothermal energy. There are now five geothermal power plants operating at Miravalles.

Top left Las Pailas geothermal power plant **Top center** Fumarole, Volcán Poás **Top right** Volcán Turrialba

In 2011, Costa Rica tapped into an additional energy source in Curubandé de Liberia, near Volcán Rincón de la Vieja, with the addition of a second plant in 2019.

The Challenge

Considering all the benefits, it seems like a no-brainer for the country to expand its capacity for geothermal power. However, there is a significant obstacle: geothermal energy is location specific, which means the plants must be built in areas where the energy is accessible. In Costa Rica's case, most of these areas are contained within national parks. As such, they are designated for recreation, education and conservation. And they are legally protected from commercial use.

> Geothermal energy is a renewable resource. It is relatively clean, producing little waste or byproduct. It is – arguably – the ultimate 'green' energy.

The Costa Rican power company ICE and other geothermal advocates are trying to find compromises (or to change the legislation). But the Ministry of Environment and Energy is dead against it, arguing that it sets a dangerous precedent for commercial exploitation of a public natural resource. It's a legitimate point, which highlights the fact that no resource is unlimited and no activity is inconsequential. Saving the planet is never simple, but every small step helps.

Five Active Volcanoes

▶ **Volcán Arenal** (p118) It's not safe to go to the crater, but you can hike along the lava flows of past eruptions.

▶ **Volcán Irazú** (p68) At 3400m, this is Costa Rica's highest volcano, topped with green crater lakes.

▶ **Volcán Poás** (p55) Has one of the largest active volcano craters in the world. Since 2017 it has been active, so strict safety measures are in place.

▶ **Volcán Rincón de la Vieja** (p140) It's not safe to go to the crater, but there is plenty of geothermal power on display in Las Pailas sector.

▶ **Volcán Turrialba** Intense activity means that the surrounding park and trails have closed frequently since 2016.

20 Find the Wild
THINGS

WILDLIFE | PHOTO OPS | VOLUNTEER

Want to watch howler monkeys swing through the trees or glimpse the smile of a sloth? On the outskirts of La Fortuna, private nature reserves are allowing wildlife to reclaim the territory and inviting visitors to take a peek. Here are some opportunities to see wild animals in their natural habitat and to learn about keeping wildlife wild.

JUAN CARLOS VINDAS/GETTY IMAGES ©

🗺 **How To**

Getting here/around
You'll need a car to get to most of these wildlife destinations, which are all located on the outskirts of La Fortuna.

How much A two-hour guided daytime walk costs around US$30, while a night walk starts at US$48.

The tour/volunteer experience at the rescue center is US$60.

Reservations Required for guided tours.

Protect yourself Always wear close-toed shoes to protect from snakes and insects. Don't forget a rain jacket and insect repellent!

TYLER WENZEL/SHUTTERSTOCK ©

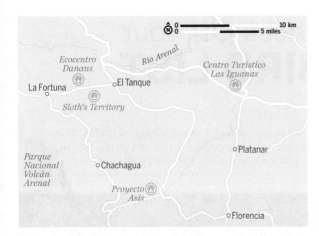

Top left Three-toed sloth **Bottom left** Red-eyed tree frog

Spot a sloth Support a reforestation effort and see the national symbol at **Sloth's Territory**, a private reserve 5km east of La Fortuna. Expert guides have an amazing ability to locate these charismatic creatures, even when they are camouflaged amid the leaves high above. Their scopes ensure that you will get a good look too.

Iguana bridge Drive 20km east to Muelle, where Rte 35 takes a sharp turn to cross a narrow bridge. Here, a mess of green iguanas hangs out in the trees above the river. Some of them are massive. You can walk across the bridge or get a good look from the **Centro Turístico Las Iguanas**. This is also a good place to grab lunch or ice cream before your next stop.

Rescue operation About 24km south of La Fortuna in San Carlos, **Proyecto Asis** is a rescue center that rehabilitates animals for release back into the wild. The goal here is to educate visitors about the importance of keeping wildlife wild. While the animals are endearing and the tour is mildly interesting, the highlight is the 'volunteer' part of the experience, when guests help to prepare the food and make animal enrichment toys for the animals.

Creatures of the night Almost every nature preserve offers a night tour to show off the frogs and spiders and insects – and even some mammals – that only come out at night. **Ecocentro Danaus** seems to specialize in frogs, including that other much sought after national symbol, the red-eyed tree frog.

🐾 Sloth Hangout

For the untrained eye, it is not easy to spot a sloth: one trick is knowing where to look. In Costa Rica, most animal lovers can tell you that the best place to look for a sloth is a cecropia tree, known locally as guarumo. Sloths like to suck on the spongey interior of the cecropia stalks (which happen to have hallucinogenic properties). And wouldn't you know it? They often fall asleep there too. Fortunately for us, the leaves are not as dense as some other trees, which gives us a chance to get a peek.

■ **Tip from Alex Araya Carvajal**, *sloth guide* at Bogarin Trail 📷 bogarintrail

21
Check Off Your
BIRD LIST

BIRDS | BIRDS | BIRDS

▬▬▬ Does your heart flutter at the sight of a new feathered friend? Follow this itinerary – traversing rainforest, cloud forest, dry forest and wetlands – to see how many of the country's 900 species you can check off your bird list.

MALLARDG500/
GETTY IMAGES ©

🗺️ Trip Notes

Getting here/around If only we could be like the birds and fly into these avian habitats. Instead, you'll need your own wheels (preferably 4WD).

When to go While birding in Costa Rica is fabulous any time of year, the bird life is more concentrated during the dry season (December to April).

Guide the way Hire a guide and see more species. Most guides travel with a scope, and they can talk to the birds.

🐦 Garden Variety

A little-known birding spot is in La Unión de Guápiles at **Donde Cope**, the private home of José 'Cope' Pérez, bird-lover and artist. His garden is hung with fruit and feeders, attracting a huge variety of avian species. Observe the action from the blind without disturbing your subjects.

■ **Tip from Geiner Huertas Reyes,** *Nature Guide at Best Chocolate*
📷 *cr_best_chocolate*

03 An early morning boat trip in the **Caño Negro Wildlife Refuge** will show off loads of water birds, including kingfishers (pictured right), herons, rails and jacanas, not to mention the smiling caimans lurking in the water.

04 With a bird list that is 350 species long, **Laguna del Lagarto Lodge** is legendary among birders. Located in Boca Tapada, which is a nesting area for the great green macaw.

01 When in Monteverde, birders head to **Curi-Cancha Reserve** to catch a glimpse of the three-wattled bellbird. He is easy to hear but difficult to see! The resplendent quetzal (pictured opposite) is also here from December to May.

02 In dry season waterfowl and shorebirds congregate around the lakes and marshes at **Palo Verde Biological Station**. You may see the rare black-crowned night heron (pictured right) or the massive jabirú stork.

05 You know they're serious about birding at **La Selva Biological Station** in Puerto Viejo de Sarapiquí because the bird walk starts at 5:45am. Reserve in advance for a two-hour 'flight' into the rainforest.

40 km
20 miles

NICARAGUA

Lago de Nicaragua

Islas Solentiname

Los Chiles

Colonia Puntarenas
Caño Negro
Upala
Canalete

Refugio de Vida Silvestre Caño Negro

Bijagua
Volcán Miravalles
Volcán Tenorio
San Rafael
Parque Nacional Volcán Tenorio

Río San Juan

Refugio de Vida Silvestre Mixto Maquenque

Boca Arenal

Puerto Viejo de Sarapiquí

Bagaces
Laguna de Arenal
Tilarán
Río Arenal
El Tanque
Pital

Corobici
Cañas
Quebrada Grande
Platanar

La Virgen
Horquetas

Parque Nacional Palo Verde
Santa Elena
Monteverde
Parque Nacional Volcán Arenal
Aguas Zarcas
La Unión de Guápiles

Santa Clara
Donde Cope

Golfo de Nicoya
Parque Nacional Braulio Carrillo

Volcán Barva

Cordillera Central

SAN JOSÉ ✪

FROM TOP: KAREL CERNY/SHUTTERSTOCK ©, RICHARD CONSTANTINOFF/SHUTTERSTOCK ©

BIRD BRIGADE

01 Scarlet macaw
This big beauty has made an amazing comeback since the 1980s, and is now easy to spot along the southern Pacific coast.

02 Blue-crowned motmot
Commonly sighted, but uncommonly gorgeous. One of six species of motmot found in Costa Rica – all of them pretty spectacular.

03 Montezuma oropendola
You'll hear the distinctive gurgling call before you see this handsome blackbird, named for the Aztec Emperor.

04 Great green macaw
Critically endangered and stridently protected, but sometimes possible to spot in all its spectacular plumage in Sarapiquí and Boca Tapada.

05 Clay-colored thrush
Not much to look at, but it sings a lovely, melodic song. And it is the national bird of Costa Rica.

06 Coppery-headed emerald hummingbird
Of the country's 50 species of hummingbird, this is one of two that are endemic to Costa Rica.

07 Resplendent quetzal
Resplendent, indeed. Depending on the season, look for them in the cloud forests around Monteverde or Providencia de Dota.

08 Three-wattled bellbird
Another cloud forest favorite, this elusive and odd-looking cotinga gives itself away with its metallic call.

09 Ornate hawk eagle
The most distinctive of the country's three hawk eagles, due to its spiky crest and bold, barred plumage.

10 Keel-billed toucan
Toucan Sam – with the rainbow-colored beak – is the most colorful of the six species of toucans that live in Costa Rica.

22 Run the RÍO

RAPIDS | NATURE | ADVENTURE

The rivers are the lifeline of the Northern Lowlands, watering the fertile farmlands, transporting the produce and providing endless entertainment for adventure seekers and wildlife-watchers. Whether you float among the flora and fauna on the Río Puerto Viejo, ride the rapids on the Sarapiquí or just go for a dip, a day on the river is a day to relish and remember.

GABBRO/ALAMY STOCK PHOTO ©

🛶 How To

Getting here/around
The tour companies offer transportation from hotels and lodges in the area.

When to go The rapids run fastest at the end of the rainy season (say, November or December) or anytime that it's been raining.

How much Rafting and floating trips run US$60 to US$80 per person.

Lunch break Stop for lunch at Rancho Magallanes for succulent chicken, roasted in a brick oven and served with tortillas and banana salsa.

MARCO LISSONI/SHUTTERSTOCK ©

Top left White-water rafting, Río Sarapiquí **Bottom left** Iguana

White-water rafting For a fantastic day out on the water, you can't beat riding the rapids on the **Río Sarapiquí**, guaranteed to get your body moving and your heart racing. Most rafting trips take place on 14km of 'extreme' white water near the town of San Miguel. Here you'll find Class II-III rapids, giving novice and experienced wave runners a thrill ride. The rapids are broken by natural pools where you can jump from cliffs, cool off with a swim and gear up for the next run. Trips on Class IV rapids are also available for more experienced wave riders.

Wildlife-watching For a more serene adventure, the same rafts (or canoes or inner tubes) go floating down the **Río Puerto Viejo**, with passengers on the lookout for birds and animals that inhabit the lush surrounding forest. The variety of water birds is incredible, not to mention stoic caimans, playful otters, sleepy sloths, two kinds of monkeys, and countless iguanas sunning themselves on the muddy riverbanks.

Excellent companies offering both kinds of trips include **Green Rivers** in Puerto Viejo de Sarapiquí, **Aventuras de Sarapiquí** in Chilamate and **Sarapiquí Outdoor Center** in La Virgen.

Take a Dip

The Northern Lowlands are steaming hot, and there's no better way to beat the heat than to take a dip in the glorious cooling waters of the **Río Sarapiquí**. Access the river from the road to Linda Vista (which is also the road to Chilamate Rainforest Retreat). After crossing the bridge, look on the left side of the road for the path down to the river. A small sandy beach and a rope swing make for a perfect picnic and swimming spot.

■ Tip from **Lluvia, Aeden and Kiara Azofeifa, and Samantha Reyes,** *resident kids at Chilamate Rainforest Retreat* @*chilamaterainforestretreat*

23

Head in the
CLOUDS

HIKING | ECOLOGY | BIRDSONG

▬▬▬ Swirling with mist, echoing with birdsong and literally dripping with life, the tropical cloud forest is an environment unlike any other. If you have ever wondered what it's like to walk (or fly) through the clouds, Santa Elena is your chance to find out. Slow your steps for a sensory overload, or pick up the pace for an adrenaline rush. Or do both.

JORDI CAMI/ALAMY STOCK PHOTO ©

🗺 How To

Getting here/around
Both Santa Elena Cloud Forest Reserve and Selvatura offer transportation to/from area hotels.

How much Admission to Santa Elena is US$18 for adults, US$12 for students and US$9 for children; the Selvatura canopy tour is US$63 for adults, US$44 for children aged 4 to 12.

Top tip If you can't see much from the observation tower, wait around. Clouds come and go, as do the views.

MILAN ZYGMUNT/SHUTTERSTOCK ©

NATURE'S CHARM/SHUTTERSTOCK ©

Feast for the senses All your senses are in for a treat at the **Santa Elena Cloud Forest Reserve**, from the lush greenery and ethereal bird calls to the ever-encroaching humidity. The place is dense with life, and the slower you go, the more you notice. Keep your eye out for high-profile highland bird species, including the resplendent quetzal, the three-wattled bellbird, the long-tailed mannakin and the emerald toucanet. A guide also helps, but there is plenty to see and hear if you prefer to go it alone. Just take your time. There are 12km of well-marked trails of varying difficulty and length. Finish up with a stop at the observation tower, which on a clear day yields a view of four volcanoes.

Boost for the heartrate For a different perspective on the cloud forest, pick up the speed and go soaring through the canopy at **Selvatura**. This high-speed canopy tour is a favorite among kids (aged four and up) and anyone who appreciates a good adrenaline rush. One of the larger zipline courses in town, Selvatura has 13 cables (plus a Tarzan swing for extra fun) strung out over an incredible stretch of primary cloud forest. Because Selvatura is right next door to the Santa Elena reserve, it has magnificent, unbroken cloud forest views – not to mention the highest altitude for a zipline course. So if you want to fly through the clouds, this is the place to do it.

Top left Santa Elena Cloud Forest Reserve **Bottom left** Emerald toucanet **Above** Ziplining, Monteverde Cloud Forest

 Cloud Coffee

Since the cloud forest awakens at dawn, the earlier you can get here, the better. The Santa Elena reserve opens at 7am, but you can come even earlier if you book the sunrise experience. It will still be dark when you arrive and make your way to the observation tower – just in time to watch the sunrise. Enjoy hot coffee and breakfast treats while you see, hear and feel the cloud forest come alive.

24 Foodie RICA

DRINK | FOOD | VIEWS

▬▬▬▬ When you grow weary of eating rice and beans, get a taste of the surprisingly sophisticated dining scene in Monteverde and Santa Elena. The focus on local ingredients, innovative preparations and fantastic settings are sure to sate your appetite and delight your senses. Each of these restaurants offers an eating experience that you won't get anywhere else.

SAN LUCAS TREETOP DINING EXPERIENCE - WWW.SANLUCAS.CR ©

🗺 How To

Getting here/around
These restaurants are within walking distance of downtown Santa Elena or Monteverde.

When to go For dinner, book a table for 5pm or 5:30pm to enjoy the scenery in the late-afternoon glow. Reservations recommended for El

Jardín and San Lucas Dining Experience.

Get your drink on Farm to Table Escondida offers beverages from its on-site 'fermentation lab,' while Stella's carries beer from Monteverde Brewery. El Jardín offers a short menu of specialty cocktails made with local fruits. Cheers!

GABBRO/ALAMY STOCK PHOTO ©

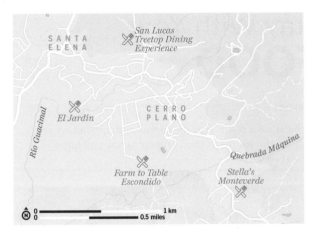

Breakfast with the birds Whether you go for a 'forest omelet' with locally foraged mushrooms or a 'tropical bowl' with seasonal fruit and homemade granola, take it out to the back patio for breakfast with the birds. Lots of multicolored species show up at **Stella's Monteverde**, including mot mots and toucanets. Capuchin monkeys tend to pass through midmorning. Later in the day, you might opt for homemade pasta or quiche and see who joins you.

Garden party You'll dine on fantastic gourmet fare, surrounded by hanging greenery and blooming fleurs at **El Jardín**, the acclaimed restaurant at Monteverde Lodge and Gardens. The greenhouse setting is a delight – especially when the orchids are abloom (January to April). Vegetarians will be in heaven with the plant-based menus. Even meat eaters will want to get in on the avocado salad with mixed beans and mango.

Locavore's delight You want local? **Farm to Table Escondida** grows most of its ingredients right here on site. The result is irresistible fresh salads and brick-oven pizzas. While you're here, you can explore the lovely grounds and gardens to see where your meal came from. (And if you're into it, the permaculture and farm tour is extremely interesting and informative.) Bonus: stunning views over the 'hidden valley,' especially at sunset.

Top left San Lucas Treetop Dining Experience **Bottom left** Stella's Monteverde

Dining in the Sky

High up on a hillside overlooking Santa Elena, eight glass pods are suspended in the sky, looking down through the clouds to the world below. Here, **San Lucas Treetop Dining Experience** promises (and delivers) a 'gastronomic adventure.' The menu is a secret – a multicourse extravaganza that celebrates the region and the country. Every course tells a story, through which diners learn about the geography and cuisine and culture of Costa Rica. The food and the setting are truly unique. There are two seatings per night: go for the early one.

25
Play With Your
FOOD

FOOD | FARMS | SUSTAINABILITY

▬▬▬▬ Tantalize your tastebuds with some Tico specialties and find out where they come from. Go straight to the source at local organic farms and hone your skills with some hands-on harvesting.

MARA VORHEES/LONELY PLANET ©

🗺 Trip Notes

Getting here/around Most *fincas* (farms) and facilities are in rural locations, so a car is essential.

How much Most tours cost between US$25 and US$35, including a generous degustation. The ranch tour is US$60 including lunch.

Reservations Book tours in advance, especially during the high season.

Souvenirs Consumables make excellent souvenirs (and gifts). Load up on chocolate, coffee and other goodies at the on-site shops at Best Chocolate and Mi Cafecito.

ⓘ **Choco-History**

Cacao has been a critical product in Costa Rica since pre-Columbian times. Cacao beans were used as currency (as recently as the 1930s) and *la hora de chocolate* (chocolate hour) was an evening ritual. In the 1980s, a blight devastated the country's cacao production. Today, production is on the rise again, as scientists work to develop disease-resistant varieties.

NICARAGUA

05 Learn how **Rancho Margot** – a self-sustaining off-the-grid ranch in El Castillo – produces its own food and electricity.

02 In Chilamate, **Costa Rica Best Chocolate** shares the process of creating the world's favorite delicacy. Visitors help with every step, especially the taste tests.

Río San Carlos

Río Tres Amigos

Río Toro

El Castillo
Río Arenal
La Fortuna
El Tanque
Boca Arenal
Pital
Puerto Viejo de Sarapiquí
Volcán Arenal
Chachagua
Platanar
Río Cuarto
La Virgen
Laguna de Arenal
Parque Nacional Volcán Arenal
Aguas Zarcas
Venecia
Zona Protectora La Selva
Horquetas
Ciudad Quesada
Colonie del Toro
San Miguel
Volcán Platanar
Parque Nacional Volcán Poás
Río Sarapiquí
Parque Nacional Braulio Carrillo
Santa Clara
Volcán Porvenir
Zarcero
Volcán Poás
Volcán Barva

04 Experience life on the farm – as in harvesting the fruits and vegetables and using them to prepare a fresh, tasty, traditional lunch – at **Finca Paraíso Organico** in La Fortuna.

01 At **Palmitour** in Horquetas, you'll discover that hearts of palm – or *palmitos* – are more delicious and versatile than you ever imagined. Tour the plantation and sample the goods.

03 How does the little red berry become a dark steaming cup of coffee? Find out at the **Mi Cafecito** (pictured opposite) coffee cooperative in San Miguel de Sarapiquí.

Golfo de Nicoya

N
0
0
20 miles
40 km

26 Waterfall MAGIC

HIKING | SWIMMING | ADVENTURE

There are a *lot* of waterfalls in Costa Rica – from gentle streams to powerful ragers, rushing over rocks or dropping down cliffs. Best of all, many of these beauties end in enticing swimming holes. If you don't swim under at least one waterfall while you are in Costa Rica, you are doing it wrong. Take your pick from one of these irresistibly swimmable *cataratas*.

KRYSSIA CAMPOS/GETTY IMAGES ©

🖼 How To

Getting here/around
Any bus traveling this part of the Interamericana can drop you at the turnoff to Llanos de Cortés, 5km north of Bagaces, from where it's a 1.5km walk to the waterfall. A shuttle to El Tigre from Santa

Elena hotels is US$10 per person. If you are driving yourself, you'll want a 4WD to get to Viento Fresco or El Tigre.

How much Admission to Llanos de Cortés is US$7, while Viento Fresco is US$17. Admission to El Tigre starts at US$29 for adults, US$19 for kids.

KIM HAMMAR/ALAMY STOCK PHOTO ©

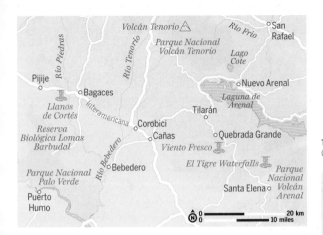

Top left Llanos de Cortés **Bottom left** Catarata El Tobogan, Viento Fresco

Llanos de Cortés Just north of Bagaces, this is one of the widest, most welcoming waterfalls you will find. A short but steep trail leads from the parking lot down to a cascade of loveliness, 28m high and 12m wide, dropping into a tranquil pond. It's a picture-perfect swimming hole with a sandy beach for your picnicking pleasure. (Bring your lunch, as there is no food for sale here.)

Viento Fresco A perfect place to break up the drive between La Fortuna and Monteverde. The hiking trail is steep and sometimes precarious. But it leads past three picturesque waterfalls of varying sizes, with one more within view in the distance. The highlight is the 75m **Arco Iris**, which casts a rainbow in the lower right corner of the pool. You can climb up behind the cascade and jump off the rocks on the right side. Scary, but not as scary as it looks!

El Tigre An adventurous and sometimes challenging 8km hike that includes four gushing falls, 10 hanging bridges and countless swimming holes along the way. The trail is well marked but often muddy, so wear your boots. If you want to avoid the uphill slog on the way back, spring for the 'full package' admission price, which includes a ride back on horseback or by 4WD. This is an all-day outing from Santa Elena.

🏊 Waterfall Swimming Safety Tips

Waterfalls and plunge pools are fluid (obviously). That means that the conditions may change dramatically, especially depending on recent rainfall. It's important to assess the risk each time you swim at any given location:

▶ Always comply with posted warnings and restrictions.

▶ If your guide says it's safe, it's probably safe.

▶ Check for underwater hazards and adequate depth before jumping into plunge pools.

▶ Be careful of currents that can force swimmers into rocks or boulders.

▶ Be cautious about swimming directly under the waterfall, as the weight of the water can be bone crushing, depending on the level of water flow.

27

La Vida
VOLCANO

GEOLOGY | ADVENTURE | HIKING

Volcán Rincón de la Vieja is one of Costa Rica's most active volcanoes, with sizeable eruptions as recently as 2022. While it's too dangerous to hike to the crater, you can still witness the volcanic activity – gurgling mud pots, steaming fumaroles and boiling hot springs – in the surrounding national park.

How To

Getting here/around
It helps to have your own wheels. Otherwise, tours run from Liberia and from beach towns on the Península de Nicoya.

When to go Las Pailas sector is closed Monday; Santa María sector closed Tuesday and Wednesday. Subject to change.

How much The US$16 park fee covers admission to both sectors on the same day (credit-card payment only). It's US$25 to soak at Río Negro. La Leona tours start at US$25.

Rainy-day blues Heavy rains cause the pools at Los Coyotes to lose their blue-green glow.

Volcanic Power on View

At **Parque Nacional Rincón de La Vieja**, near Curubandé de Liberia, take a walk around Las Pailas sector to get a glimpse of the furious energy that is roiling just beneath the surface of the earth. The hiking trail **Sendero Las Pailas** is only 3.5km, but it bubbles with multihued fumaroles, tepid springs and steaming, flatulent mud pots, as well as a young and feisty *volcancito* (small volcano). You can't go to the crater, but this trail gives you a pretty good idea of what's going on up there. The park opens at 8am. Arrive early to beat the tour buses coming up from the coast.

If you want more, you might spend the better part of a day in the national park, as there are two additional trails (9km to 10km each) leading to scenic but unswimmable waterfalls.

The Lookout

For a perfect end to a perfect day, head to **El Mirador** (The Lookout) in Cañas Dulces for traditional food and spectacular views over the Guanacaste lowlands. The westward facing panorama is grand at anytime, but sunsets are glorious. Cañas Dulces is about 11km west of Curubandé.

Top left Fumarole, Parque Nacional Rincón de La Vieja **Top right** hiking, Parque Nacional Rincón de La Vieja **Bottom left** Crater, Parque Nacional Rincón de La Vieja

Soothing Soak

There's no better way to recover from a volcano hike, than a hot-spring soak. Let that same thermal power soothe your muscles and restore your energy. The most popular option is to stop at **Río Negro Hot Springs** on the way out of the park. This privately run endeavor offers nine pools in a scenic setting on the Río Negro. The thermally heated water is pumped into small, stone-built pools and cooled to varying temperatures, with access

to the river to cool off. The facility provides towels, lockers and showers, but you'll want to bring water shoes for the river.

For a more rustic and all-natural experience, drive 30 minutes east to the **Santa María sector** of Parque Nacional Rincón de la Vieja. Here, a trail leads 3km through the 'enchanted forest,' past a lovely waterfall to sulfurous hot springs, or *aguas termales*. Surrounded by the tropical forest, you can soak in two rocky pools – crafted and heated

ⓘ Secluded Spot in Curubandé

Our favorite Sunday destination is on Río Blanco, near the bridge where locals picnic. We usually head down the river to a more hidden spot, for swimming and rock jumping. Or – if you're a little crazy (like Pablo) – you can jump in from the tree! A bit farther, there's another 'secret' swimming area, with a rock that forms a natural (cold-water) jacuzzi. We have spent many Sundays swimming and soaking there. We always spot blue morpho butterflies, birds, iguanas and sometimes even monkeys.

From the Mini Super in Curubandé, head west out of town for 1.6km, until you reach the bridge. Our secluded spot is down the river to the left (west).

■ Tip from
Pablo Camacho Calvo and Sara Garrett,
Un Tico y Una Gringa Tours
ⓘ *untico_unagringatours*

NORTHERN COSTA RICA EXPERIENCES

FAR LEFT: HEMIS/ALAMY STOCK PHOTO ©;
LEFT: ALEXEY STIOP/SHUTTERSTOCK ©

by Mother Earth – and cool off in the stream. Rain dilules the pools, so you may have cooler temperatures, depending on when you go.

River Canyon Adventure

Book in advance for a guided hike to **La Leona Waterfall**, one in a series of waterfalls along the Río Blanco near Curubandé de Liberia. Although it's called 'White River', it's actually heavenly blue, due to mineral deposits on the river bed. The exhilarating hike through the canyon features river crossings, rock climbing, cavern crawling and cliff jumping – if you so dare. You'll pass three waterfalls on the way, including one glorious cascade that is hidden inside a cavern. Be advised that you will get completely soaked! (Waterproof hiking sandals are best.)

Left Río Negro Hot Springs **Below** Turquoise-browed motmot

28 Forest Green &
RIVER BLUE

SWIMMING | HIKING | WILDLIFE

From the dreamy blue waters of the namesake river to the deep greens of the surrounding forests, the Río Celeste region shimmers with vibrant, colorful life. Spend a day hiking and swimming amid the technicolor landscape, and stay for the night to see what lurks in the blackness.

🗺️ How To

Getting here/around
You'll need a vehicle to reach the national park, as well as Tapir Valley.

How much Admission to the national park is US$12. The night tour at Tapir Valley is US$67 (cash only).

Muddy waters Heavy rains may dilute the water of the Río Celeste and stir up mud – causing the river to lose its dreamy blue hue.

Celestial Falls

The **Parque Nacional Volcán Tenorio** is a cool, misty, magical place, covered by cloud forests and teeming with life. Soaring 1916m above the forest is the park's namesake volcano. Below, is the glorious Río Celeste, which winds its way through the park in a series of waterfalls and lagoons.

A hiking trail leads from the entrance, showing off some of the river's highlights. You'll pass the **Catarata de Río Celeste**, a milky-blue waterfall that cascades 30m down the rocks into a fantastically aquamarine pool. Stop at the *mirador* (lookout point) for grand views of Tenorio from the double-decker wooden platform. Further on is the spectacular **Pozo Azul** (Blue Lagoon). The trail loops around the lagoon until you arrive at the confluence of rivers known as **Los Teñideros**

ⓘ Why is the River So Blue?

The ethereal color of the Río Celeste is an optical illusion, caused by certain volcanic minerals suspended in the water. The water acts as a prism and separates the color waves as usual. But the mineral particles reflect the blue waves, giving the water its azure appearance.

Top left Río Celeste **Top right** Parque Nacional Volcán Tenorio **Bottom left** Pozo Azul

(The Dyers). Here, two small rivers mix together to create the blueberry milk of Río Celeste. It's quite a display.

The out-and-back trail is about 5km round-trip, but some parts of the trail are steep (and most parts are muddy). You'll want your boots.

Pearly Blue Pools

Swimming is strictly forbidden everywhere in the national park. But the river's luscious blue is irresistible, and if you want to submerse yourself in these enticing waters, you have a few options. From the park entrance, drive about 1km east to the first bridge. Here, a rough trail leads down to the river's edge. Known as the **Río Celeste free pool**, this is a popular spot for a post-hike dip. The other option is right next door at **Cabinas Piuri,** where the Río Celeste flows by in a series of sweet and swimmable pools. Non-guests pay a small fee to access the river. The water is cool, refreshing and beguilingly blue.

ⓘ Deets about Dantas

Its official name is Baird's tapir, or the Central American tapir, but locally it's known as a 'danta.'

▶ Distantly related to a horse and a rhino, this gentle giant is a herbivore that weighs in at a hefty 150kg to 300kg.

▶ Tapirs are mostly solitary, but they are monogamous with their mate.

▶ Their babies have the color and pattern of a fawn – reddish-brown with white stripes and spots.

▶ Tapirs have few natural predators, but they are endangered due to loss of habitat.

Bijagua

Tapir Valley
Nature Reserve

Cabinas Piuri

Río Celeste Free Pool

Pozo Azul
Los Teñideros

Catarata de Río Celeste

Río Tenorio

Río Frio

Volcán
Tenorio

Parque Nacional
Volcán Tenorio

10 km

5 miles

Black of Night

They say that 60% of tropical rainforest animals are nocturnal, so it's worth coming out after dark to take a look. (Of course, they are harder to see. That's the downside.) **Tapir Valley Nature Reserve** borders Volcán Tenorio national park. Book a night tour for a rare chance to see the elusive (and endangered) Baird's tapir, as well as frogs, snakes, kinkajous and other creatures of the night.

Opposite Baird's tapir **Left** Yellow Eyelash Viper **Above** Kinkajou

29 Beach
HOPPING

SWIM | SUN | SEA

▬▬▬ West of La Cruz, there is a little corner of coastal Costa Rica that is mostly untouched by international tourism. Cruise around the edge of the Golfo de Santa Elena – from Cuajiniquil to El Jobo – to discover tiny fishing villages and idyllic beaches, all surrounded by forest and farmland and spectacular views across the gulf.

GIANFRANCO VIVI/SHUTTERSTOCK ©

🗺 How To

Getting here/around
You'll need your own vehicle to explore this area.

When to go The weather is consistently dry and sunny from December to April, but there are fewer people from May to November.

How much All of the beaches are free of charge, except Playa Junquillal (part of a national park), which costs US$15 per person.

NATURE'S CHARM/SHUTTERSTOCK ©

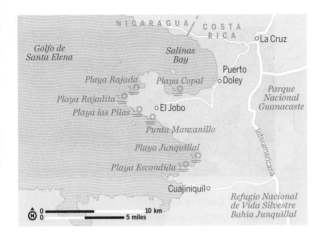

Heading from south to north from Cuajiniquil:

Playa Escondida A sweet little beach with no sign. Just offshore, a tiny island decorates the seascape and invites exploration. If you're hoping to find a deserted beach, this could be the one.

Playa Junquillal Part of the eponymous wildlife refuge, this gorgeous crescent of sand embraces a calm, quiet bay that's perfect for swimming. It's a popular spot for Tico families and iguanas. For your money, you'll get plenty of picnic tables, as well as bathrooms and showers. Two short trails (totaling 1.7km) hug the coast, traversing dry tropical forest. They lead to a marine bird lookout in one direction and to the mangroves in the other.

Punta Manzanillo The tiny beach south of El Jobo is not for swimming, but it's worth a stop to see colorful fishing boats bobbing at their lines and local fisherfolk hauling and cleaning their catch.

Playa las Pilas Off the road to Rajada, a rough road leads 500m south to this secret spot. Striated cliffs flank the rocky beach, which is otherwise surrounded by forest. It's a stunner.

Playa Rajada Lined with tree-shaded picnic tables, this long, narrow beach curves around its own bay, creating a perfect, placid swimming area. At the southern end, the outgoing tide leaves a lagoon of jumping fish and scurrying crabs. You can also sneak over to the tiny hidden **Playa Rajadita**.

Top left Playa Rajada **Bottom left** Playa Junquillal

Wind + Water

Want to ride the wind? This remote northwestern corner of Costa Rica is the country's kitesurfing capital, where euphoric riders sail across Bahía Salinas, which stretches all the way to Nicaragua. From November to May, the wind howls at 20 to 40 knots, and the surrounding hills reliably funnel it into the bay. **Playa Copal** – as wide and wild as they come – is the perfect place to catch it and go for a ride. **Kiteboarding Costa Rica** offers accommodations on the beach, as well as equipment and instruction as needed. Hang on tight!

Where History Happens

WHAT WENT DOWN AT SANTA ROSA

Now a national park, Santa Rosa in Guanacaste was a focal point for Costa Rican history in the 19th and 20th centuries. Originally a farm, a replica of the old hacienda known as La Casona still stands as a testament to the history that unfolded here.

CARL DEABREU PHOTOGRAPHY/SHUTTERSTOCK ©

Manifest Destiny Derailed

In the mid-19th century, the mercenary William Walker and his ragtag army attempted to conquer Central America, in an ill-advised effort to fulfill the 'manifest destiny' of the US. His initial foray into Mexico was a bust, but in 1855 he seized control of Nicaragua, taking advantage of the civil war raging there. Costa Rica went on high alert.

In February 1856, Costa Rican president Juan Rafael Mora Porras declared war on Nicaragua and recruited a volunteer army of some 9000 civilians to defend the northern border. The troops marched north from San José, while Walker's 'filibuster' army – composed mainly of European soldiers – came south to head them off. The Costa Rican patriots surprised the filibuster army at Santa Rosa, winning the battle in a record-breaking 14 minutes.

A month later, the Costa Rican fighters penetrated into Nicaraguan territory and dealt another blow to Walker's men at the Second Battle of Rivas, where Juan Santamaría became a national hero (p50).

Nonetheless, Walker declared himself president of Nicaragua and the so-called Filibuster War continued for another year. But the Central American military coalition – led by Costa Rica – finally drove him out in May 1857 (and he was later executed in Honduras).

Cold War in the Hot Tropics

The 20th century also saw Yankee meddling in Central American affairs – in the very place where Costa Rica had so ably defended its independence 123 years earlier. In 1979 the rebellious Sandinistas toppled the American-backed Somoza

Top left La Casona **Top center** Juan Rafael Mora Porras **Top right** El Avión

dictatorship in Nicaragua. Alarmed by the Sandinistas' Soviet and Cuban ties, fervently anticommunist US president Ronald Reagan moved to support the Contra rebels who were inciting civil war in Nicaragua. The organizational details of the counterrevolution were delegated to Oliver North, a junior officer working out of the White House basement. He dubbed the campaign 'Project Democracy.'

Under intense US pressure, Costa Rica was dragged in. The Contras set up camp in northern Costa Rica, from where they staged guerrilla raids. Clandestine CIA operatives and US military advisors assisted the effort. By the mid-1980s, they had built a secret airstrip in the jungle near Playa Portrero Grande (part of Parque Nacional Santa Rosa) to fly weapons and supplies into Nicaragua.

> Santa Rosa was a focal point for Costa Rican history in the 19th and 20th centuries. La Casona still stands as a testament to the history that unfolded.

In 1986 Óscar Arias Sánchez won the Costa Rican presidential election. A coffee baron and intellectual reformer, Arias had run on a platform of regional peace. Once in office, he affirmed his commitment to a negotiated resolution and reasserted Costa Rican national independence. He vowed to uphold his country's pledge of neutrality and to vanquish the Contras from its territory.

In a public ceremony, Costa Rican schoolchildren planted trees on top of the CIA's secret airfield. President Arias became the driving force in uniting Central America around a peace plan, which ended the Nicaraguan war and earned him the Nobel Peace Prize in 1987.

ⓘ Remnants of History

President Arias's Nobel Peace Prize is the most noteworthy outcome of the US-Contra affair (and lasting peace, of course). But the Ticos – and the tourists – got a few other good things out of it.

Ollie's Point Nowadays, Playa Portrero Grande is a popular surfing beach. And the wave – a long, glorious right point break – is named for none other than Oliver North.

El Avión An old US cargo plane – retired from its gun-running days – is the centerpiece of a restaurant in Manuel Antonio. Best known as 'the Contra bar' (p207).

Listings

BEST OF THE REST

Wildlife-Watching

Arenal Oasis

Awesome place for a night walk in La Fortuna, with 35 species of frogs as well as other nocturnal creatures.

Bogarin Trail

Birdwatching and sloth spotting on a short, flat trail, just outside of La Fortuna. If you have your heart set on seeing a sloth, you should definitely spring for the guide.

Frog's Heaven

Here – in Las Horquetas – reside the most colorful frog species, including the red-eyed tree frog. Make a reservation for a tour to spot not only frogs, but bats, sloths and more.

La Selva Biological Station

A celebrated research station and wildlife reserve south of Puerto Viejo de Sarapiquí. Guided hikes will introduce you to some of the hundreds of species of resident birds, mammals and insects.

Monkey Park

White-faced capuchin monkeys are often sighted here, as well as frogs, anteaters and other rainforest friends. Located about 19km east of La Fortuna. Insect repellent is essential.

Monteverde Cloud Forest Reserve

The original cloud forest reserve, founded by Quakers in 1972.

Santuario Ecológico Monteverde

A smallish sanctuary amid premontane forest and farmland. Hike on untrodden trails to spot coatis and birds and to cool off beneath a 30m waterfall.

Tirimbina Rainforest Center

Situated 2km from La Virgen, this is a working environmental research and education center, with 9km of trails, a cacao plantation and a range of interesting wildlife tours.

Animal Encounters & Garden Tours

Butterfly Conservatory

The highlight of this facility in El Castillo is the enclosed habitats, fluttering with dozens of species of butterflies. But there are also botanical gardens, hiking trails and wonderful volcano views.

Jardín de Mariposas

In Monteverde, four gardens represent different habitats – altogether home to 40-some species of butterflies (and plenty of other insects). Witness the whole fascinating life cycle.

Bat Jungle

A small but super-informative exhibit – home to almost 100 free-flying bats. Learn all about echolocation, bat wing aerodynamics and other amazing flying-mammal facts.

Postman butterfly

Jardín de Orquídeas

Shady trails wind past more than 500 types of orchids at the Orchid Garden in Santa Elena. See some rare species and learn how to keep your orchids at home beautiful and blooming.

Hot Springs

Tabacón Hot Springs

The only hot-springs resort in La Fortuna that is built around Río Choillin, the actual free-flowing nature-made river that is warmed by the volcano (in addition to its human-made pools).

The Springs Resort

The biggest hot-springs facility in La Fortuna, with 25 thermal pools of varying temperatures, a couple of swim-up bars and more.

Río Perdido

A high-end resort in Bagaces, with luxurious (but very sulphur-smelling) riverside pools, heated by Volcán Miravalles.

Las Hornillas

A unique family-owned place in Miravalles that includes a walkway through fumaroles and bubbling mud pots, in addition to the volcano-heated pools and mud bath.

Canyon de la Vieja

On the banks of the Río Colorado, this lodge has a series of thermal pools, plus a full-service spa and a glorious river swimming area.

Lakes & Waterways

Arenal Kayaks

Explore the Laguna de Arenal from the seat of a kayak, with plenty of wildlife-watching and swimming stops along the way.

Green Rivers

The ever-amiable couple Kevín and Evelyn Martínez offer a wide variety of rafting and kayaking tours, from family-friendly floats to adrenaline-pumping rapid rides.

Tabacón Hot Springs

Aventuras del Sarapiquí

Located right on the river in Chilamate, this outfit offers land, air and water adventures. In addition to white-water rafting, there's canoeing, horseback riding and a canopy tour on site.

Sarapiquí Outdoor Center

Owner David Duarte is a local paddling authority in La Virgen. In addition to rafting excursions, SOC offers kayak rental and lessons.

Canopy Tours

100% Aventura

This operation in Santa Elena boasts the longest zipline in Latin America, as well as a Tarzan swing, a 15m rappel, two Superman ziplines and a network of suspension bridges.

Arenal Mundo Aventura

This all-in-one adventure park has one of the best canopy tours in La Fortuna, as well as a waterfall rappelling and horseback riding adventure.

Mistico Hanging Bridges

Explore the rainforest and canopy at a peaceful pace, via six suspended bridges and 10 traditional bridges, along a single 3km trail near Laguna de Arenal.

Monteverde Extremo

This place has a canopy ride that allows you to fly Superman-style through the air, the highest and most adrenaline-addled Tarzan swing in the area, and a bungee jump from 150m. One way or another, you will scream.

Sky Adventures

All zipline and hanging-bridges tours include a gondola ride up to the top of the course. Locations in Santa Elena and El Castillo (near Arenal).

 Learn Something New

Costa Rica Cooking

Learn to make *empanadas* (turnovers stuffed with meat or cheese), ceviche or other Costa Rican classics – then enjoy the fruits of your labor. In La Fortuna.

CPI Spanish School

Monteverde Spanish School offering language courses and lodging with local families for all levels, as well as more specialized courses.

 Casados, **Ceviche y Más**

La Ventanita $

Fabulously tasty *chifrijo* (rice and beans in a bowl with fried pork pieces), as well as burritos, tacos and *batidos* (fruit shakes) in El Castillo. All tables have an incredible view of Arenal.

Jalapas $$

Perched high above La Fortuna, this excellent restaurant offers modern interpretations of traditional food, served in a spectacular setting. Choose between volcano views to the south and panoramic vistas of the lowlands in the north.

El Chante Verde $

Bright and inviting, this place is on the road to the waterfalls near La Fortuna. The menu is full of fresh salads and bowls, well-stuffed sandwiches and refreshing fruit drinks.

El Cacao $

Sadly, there is no chocolate on the menu at El Cacao, located at Best Chocolate in Chilamate. But there are tasty traditional dishes and intriguing pizzas, including the house special Pizza Theobrome ('food of the gods'), with chicken, shrimp and bacon.

La Cueva de Marisco $$

This unassuming place in Puerto Viejo de Sarapiquí cooks up seafood just right, offering grilled fish and scrumptious ceviche.

Hummingbird Café $

A delightful lunch spot in Bijagua de Upala, surrounded by birds, frogs and flowers. The menu is short and sweet: veggie burgers and fish tacos are highlights.

La Choza del Maíz $

A local favorite in Bijagua, this simple *soda* (small local restaurant) features the region's favorite ingredient: corn. Excellent place to try *chorreadas* (corn pancakes) or fill up on a *casado* (set meal).

Café Liberia $$

Dark coffee and gourmet food in a romantic colonial-era house in downtown Liberia. French chef Sebastian specializes in European classics, including irresistible sweet and savory crêpes.

Chifrijo

Restaurante Arrecife $$

Your perfect pitstop after a day of beach hopping. This breezy place is tucked away in the tiny village of Cuajiniquil. Look for fresh seafood and fruity cocktails, with or without the alcohol.

Bon Appétit $$$

When you have a hankering for Italian food (and wine), head to this delightful upscale eatery in Santa Elena. Handmade pasta and grilled meats are good for body and soul on a chilly evening in the cloud forest.

Brews & Booze

Purple Cow $

Your go-to coffee stop in La Fortuna. And what's coffee without a sweet treat to accompany it?

El Mercadito Arenal $$

In 'downtown' La Fortuna, this little food court has places serving sushi, tacos and pizza. The talented bartenders at the Mixology Bar keep everything (and everybody) well lubricated.

Celajes Lounge $$$

Have a sunset drink on the terrace at the Hotel Belmar in Monteverde, featuring seasonal cocktails, craft beer and sweeping views to the Pacific. *Bocas* (appetizers) served daily from 4:30pm to 5:30pm.

Monteverde Brewing Co $$

Drink fresh beer and eat burgers in the cloud forest. This newish place in Santa Elena makes six types of beer, including a rich, delicious coffee stout and a hoppy, fruity IPA.

Café Monteverde $$

This delightful cafe in Santa Elena is connected to a fantastic community-run, sustainable coffee farm and education center. Drinking coffee is a given; you might as well help save the planet while you're at it!

El Indio Desnudo $$

Tasty food, strong drinks and live music on Friday nights. This is an outdoor affair with a

Casado

casual atmosphere. Menu highlights include the Tomahawk steak and lobster Thermidor. Come hungry.

Numu Brewing Company $$

A cool craft brewery in an industrial complex opposite the Liberia airport. Very limited snacks on offer, but the beer is the real deal. Can't beat a Numu Lager on a hot day.

Souvenir Shopping

Neptune's House of Hammocks

Want to take home some of that *pura vida* vibe? Pick up a hammock or swinging chair from this little shop on the road to the waterfall near La Fortuna.

Luna Azul

In Santa Elena, this gallery is packed with hand-crafted goodies, especially stylish and stunning jewelry.

Monteverde Art House

This hub of creativity includes a wonderful boutique selling locally made products, as well as a coffee shop, gardens and an outdoor amphitheater.

Scan to find more things to do in Northern Costa Rica online

PENÍNSULA DE NICOYA

BEACHES | RAINFOREST | PARTIES

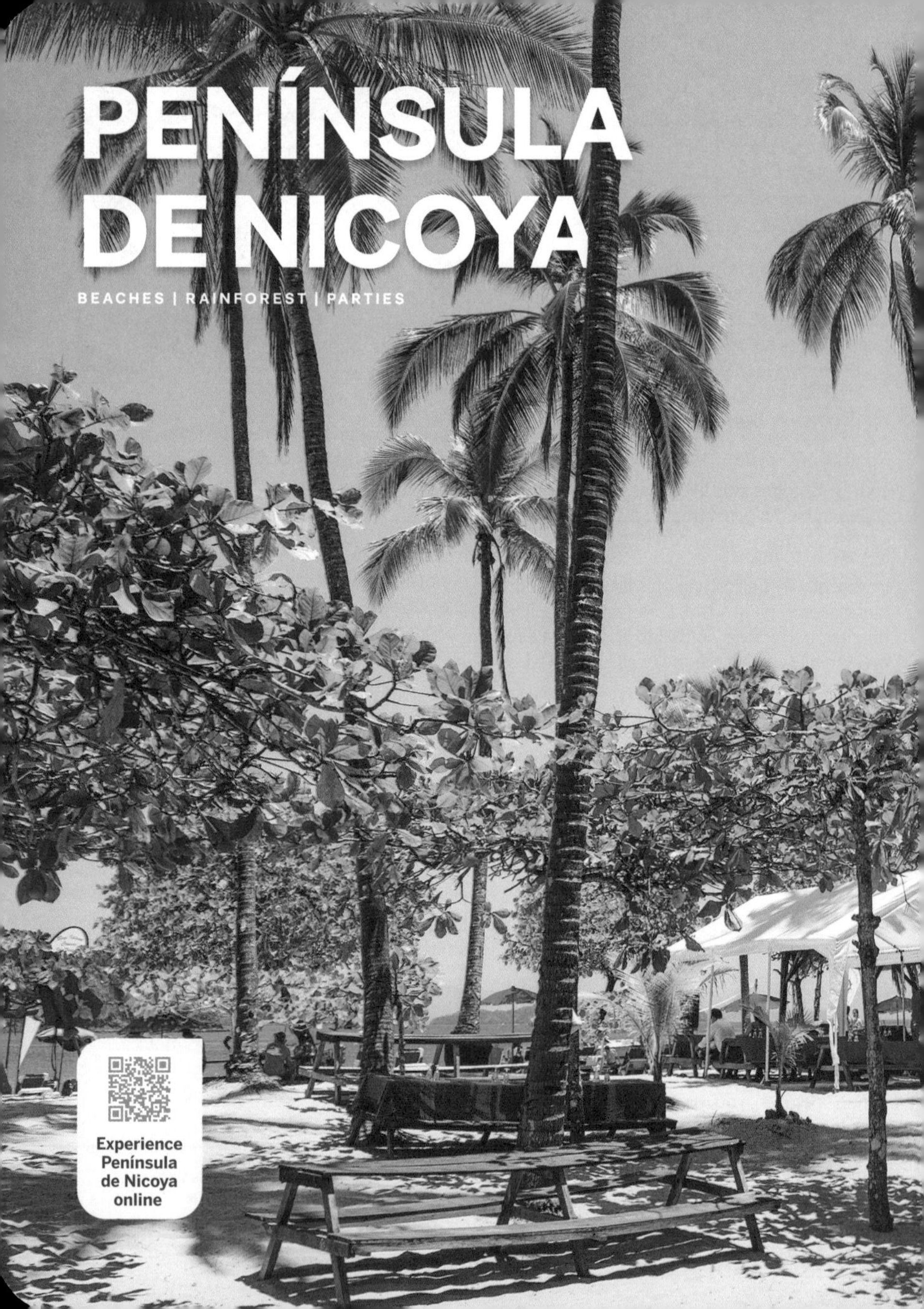

Experience
Península
de Nicoya
online

Golfo de Papagayo

Sunbathe and swim on the white sands of **Playa Conchal** (p173)
🚗 1½hr from LIR

Parque Nacional Marino Las Baulas de Guanacaste

Laguna de Arenal

Huacas
Matapalo
Villareal
Río Cañas
Santa Cruz
Guaitil

Surf all day and party all night at **Tamarindo** (p171)
🚗 2hr from LIR

Tamarindo
27 de Abril
San Antonio
Parque Nacional Barra Honda
Quebrada Honda

Paraíso

Parque Nacional Diriá
Nicoya

Marbella

Península de Nicoya

Mansión

Hojancha

Río Nosara

Witness thousands of sea turtles eggs hatching at once on **Playa Ostional** (p160)
🚗 3hr from LIR

Nosara

Santa Marta

Garza
Sámara
Carrillo
Islita
La Javilla

Paquera

San Francisco de Coyote
Pochote
Curú
Tambor
Cóbano

Kayak and snorkel at **Chora Island Reserve** (p167)
🚗 2hr from LIR

PACIFIC OCEAN

Santa Teresa
Mal País
Cabuya
Montezuma

PENÍNSULA DE NICOYA
Trip Builder

Swim at waterfalls and jump on a Tarzan swing at **Montezuma** (p167)
🚗 4hr from LIR

Surf culture with new-age hipster and hippie vibes. The beaches here boast some of the country's toughest currents and most brilliant sunsets. Celebrities, expats and backpackers come to connect with nature and the *pura vida* party scene.

Ⓝ 0 ——— 40 km
0 ——— 20 miles

Practicalities

ARRIVING

Daniel Oduber Quirós International Airport, Liberia (LIR) Caters to tourists visiting the Nicoya Península. **Juan Santamaría International Airport, San José (SJO)** Main entry point for international travelers, offers domestic flights.

CONNECT

LIR airport has free wi-fi as do most hotels and restaurants. Buy a Costa Rican SIM card to best maintain phone service.

MONEY

Booking a hotel that has breakfast included in the nightly price helps to save money. Meals are expensive in popular beach towns.

WHERE TO STAY

Town/ Village	Pro/Con
Montezuma	New-age enclave known for its epic waterfalls.
Tamarindo	Surf spot and party town catering to tourists and expats.
Nosara	Easygoing energy attracting wellness-focused travelers.
Santa Teresa	Surfers, influencers and backpackers flock here.

EATING & DRINKING

For a memorable sunset dinner on one of Nosara's magical beaches, make a reservation at La Luna. This Mediterranean restaurant is a departure from typical Costa Rican or seaside cuisine but its food is made with local ingredients and lots of love.

Always get a *batido* (fruit shake) or *agua fresca* made from fresh fruits like *sandía* (watermelon) or *piña* (pineapple). Try whatever is in season.

Best *casado* (set meal)
Rosi's Soda Tica (p180)

Must-try ceviche
La Cevicheria (p180)

GETTING AROUND

Car Renting a 4WD is necessary to navigate rough or unpaved roads and river crossings.

Bus and shuttle Public buses run from Liberia to various popular coastal points. They're cheaper but take longer. Private shuttles run from LIR airport to hotels in coastal towns, including Tamarindo, Nosara, Playas del Coco and Sámara.

JAN–APR
Peak season; crowds, higher prices; hot, sunny, minimal rain

MAY–AUG
Rainy season begins; sunny mornings, afternoon storms

SEP–OCT
Rainiest months; roads may flood; excursions may get canceled

NOV–DEC
Less rain; holiday season begins

30 Into the WILD

ANIMALS | NATURE | ADVENTURE

The wonder of Costa Rica's unique biodiversity can't be overstated, and nowhere is this more evident than on Península de Nicoya. Playa Ostional is home to the *arribada* – a mass turtle-hatching event that happens in only a handful of countries around the world. At the Curu National Wildlife Refuge, numerous ecosystems and animal species intersect for a multidimensional experience.

KRYSSIA CAMPOS/GETTY IMAGES ©

🗺 How To

Getting here Many visitors to Península de Nicoya drive rental cars. Others stay in Tamarindo or Playas del Coco and book day tours. The Curu Wildlife Refuge is a 20-minute drive from Montezuma and Paquera.

When to go Peak *arribada* season in Ostional is May through December. The biggest ones happen from September through December, coinciding with the rainy season. Early morning (5am to 6am) and sunset (5pm to 6pm) are the best times each day. Dry season is the best time to visit Curu.

FRANCESCO PUNTROL/ALAMY STOCK PHOTO ©

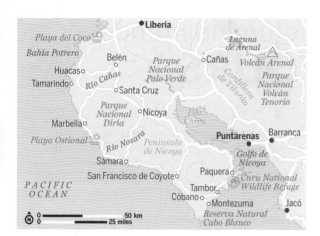

Turtle hatching When thousands of sea turtles arrive to hatch their eggs together, it's called an *arribada* – the term is derived from the Spanish word for 'arrival'. The largest *arribadas* in Costa Rica happen at **Playa Ostional** in **Refugio Nacional de Vida Silvestre Ostional**. The sea turtles are olive ridleys. These are the smallest and most abundant species, although they're still endangered due to climate change and pollution. Visitors to the refuge are required to enter with a guide. Tours can be reserved online via the Ostional Guide Association Facebook page, or in person at its office in Ostional.

Wildlife-watching If you're transiting Montezuma and the southern part of Península de Nicoya, visit the **Curu National Wildlife Refuge** for ecotourism excursions. The refuge is a remote, privately owned and managed reserve with dozens of trails through rainforests, mangrove swamps and beaches. There are over 3700 acres of protected land and hundreds of species of mammals, birds and plant life. It's a very rural community with few amenities, so most visitors stay in nearby Montezuma. However, there are a few cabins for travelers who want to spend a night (or a few) on the reserve. It's open most days from 7am until 3pm, but check SINAC.go.cr before you go to confirm.

Top and bottom left Olive ridley sea turtles, Playa Ostional

🔭 Rules for Turtle-Watching

Sea-turtle-watching is generally a passive activity, but by being on the beach, you're part of the environment and have a part to play. If you're going to watch the sea turtles nest and hatch, wear black. The mother turtles swim along the coast searching for the safest beaches to lay their eggs, and if they see bright lights and colors, they won't nest at that location. Don't use your camera flash either because the turtles are sensitive to light. The best approach is to lay low, be an observer and don't touch the turtles or get in the way.

31 Bioluminescence
TOURS

NATURE | RIVERS | KAYAKS

▬▬▬ Float amid glowing rivers to experience the incredible chemical phenomenon of bioluminescence in action. Kayak tours give visitors a front row seat from which to witness nature's nighttime magic show. When visiting southern Península de Nicoya, make time for any of the bioluminescence tours in Montezuma, Paquera, Tambor and Santa Teresa.

🗺 How To

Getting here/around If staying in Montezuma or Santa Teresa, many tours offer transportation to departure points. Brave travelers with 4WD vehicles and solid cell service can drive on their own to meet their tour guides.

When to go New moons are the best times for these night tours because there's no moon lighting up the sky. Skip September and October when rains cause flooding and dangerous conditions.

Tours Most take between 90 minutes and two hours.

Map:

0 — 20 km
0 — 10 miles
N

Playa Naranjo
Isla San Lucas
Península de Nicoya
La Javilla
San Francisco de Coyote
Paquera
Punta Cuchillo
Curú
Isla Alcatraz
Isla Tortuga
Pochote
Córbano
Tambor
Montezuma
Golfo de Nicoya
Santa Teresa
Mal País — Cabuya
Reserva Natural Cabo Blanco

What is it? Bioluminescence is the natural phenomenon that gives water and marine life a glowing appearance. Costa Rica has two main areas where visitors can kayak through bodies of bioluminescent water: Península de Nicoya and Península de Osa. Both places host the special single-celled organisms called dinoflagellates that are responsible for the awe-inspiring glow of the water. As they grow in large quantities, together they produce a chemical reaction that creates light energy and that glow-in-the-dark effect.

While bioluminescence is rare for land animals, it's extremely common in marine life. That's why it looks like you're kayaking through a river of LED lights. The calm waters of **Paquera Bay** are especially rife with these blue-green looking plankton, and are a prominent place for bioluminescence tours. A fish

🦫 Things to Bring

▶ Bug repellent, especially since you'll be out on water in the evening – mosquitos love to hang out by water and are very active after sunset.

▶ A small dry bag to carry your keys, phone or other valuables that need to stay dry. This bag comes in handy for other water adventures such as scuba diving and snorkeling. It's also a convenient way to protect your items at the beach.

▶ Clothing and shoes that can get wet.

▶ A headlamp to light the way between the beach and your car.

swimming by or you dipping a paddle in the water can generate an impromptu neon light show. **Punta Cuchillo**, near Santa Teresa, is also a prime spot for bioluminescence kayak tours.

When and how The glow can be seen all year round, although if there's been stormy weather, like during the peak of the rainy season, the waterways may be too unsafe for tours. While tours are primarily conducted in kayaks, some tour operators offer the option of a motorized boat. This is for those who may be nervous about kayaking at night or who want to take photos with a fancy, non-waterproof camera.

Above Bioluminescence kayak tour, Península de Nicoya

32 National PARKS

WILDLIFE | BIODIVERSITY | HIKING

Costa Rica offers a plethora of national parks with various types of terrain and ecosystems. Península de Nicoya's parks protect wildlife on land and in the ocean and give travelers opportunities to experience these biological marvels. Traverse jungles, rivers and historical sites to experience the variety of Costa Rica's exquisite landscapes and the creatures that populate them.

🗺 How To

Getting here A rented 4WD is necessary to visit these off-the-beaten-track parks, where you'll need to navigate dirt roads and possibly river crossings.

When to go Check at sinac.go.cr to make sure the parks are open. Many are closed on Monday and Tuesday. Dry season is the best time to go to ensure smooth roads. These parks are not massively touristed, and so may not be crowded during high season.

Parque Nacional Santa Rosa
🏛 Museo Histórico Casona de Santa Rosa
Golfo de Papagayo
El Coco
●Liberia
○Comunidad
Bahía Potrero
Huacas
Marino las Baulas de Guanacaste Tamarindo/ Playa Grande National Park
Cañas
Tamarindo
○Santa Cruz
Parque Nacional Diriá
Marbella○
Río Nosara
Península de Nicoya
Golfo de Nicoya
Garza
Bahía Garza Sámara
San Francisco de Coyote
PACIFIC OCEAN
Reserva Natural Absoluta Cabo Blanco
Santa Teresa○
Montezuma
Mal País○
Cabuya
0 ——— 40 km
0 ——— 20 miles

Reserva Natural Absoluta Cabo Blanco Just south of Montezuma, this reserve boasts remote and challenging trails with rewarding payoffs. It was established in 1963 as Costa Rica's first nature reserve. There are two trails: the 5km **Sueco Trail**, which leads to the beach; and **Danes Trail**,

a shorter 2km loop. If you want to make it to the beach, it's imperative to arrive early in the morning so you have enough time to complete the trail and play in the water. This trail is also more demanding with some steep ascents through dense rainforests and areas of loose gravel and jagged roots.

The trail ends at a stunning white-sand beach, perfect for cooling off after a 5km hike.

Parque Nacional Santa Rosa In Guanacaste, this park is a Unesco World Heritage Site and the only Protected Wilderness Area that houses a historical museum. Santa Rosa National

Above White-faced monkey **Left** Parque Nacional Santa Rosa

ⓘ A Battle for the Country's Future

The museum in Parque Nacional Santa Rosa, **Museo Histórico Casona de Santa Rosa**, is devoted to Costa Rica's small military history. The site is where Ticos defeated William Walker, a lawyer and slave owner from the US who was trying to build a slave empire along Costa Rica's Pacific coast in the 1850s. The country does not have many war heroes, but there is enormous pride in the battle that took place where Santa Rosa National Park now stands. Because of the battle, the park was established as protected land in the 1970s.

Park has the only preserved dry forest land in Central America. Visit the **Murciélago Sector** to experience the dry forest along with beaches, trails, freshwater rivers and mangroves. Although one of Costa Rica's largest parks, it's among the least visited.

Marino las Baulas de Guanacaste Tamarindo/Playa Grande National Park This park is home to the famous *baulas* or leatherback turtles, which nest and hatch here. Visitors can take guided turtle conservation tours at night, and many also go on kayak tours through the **Marino las Baulas National Park Mangrove Estuary**.

33 Swimmer's **DELIGHT**

DIVING | SNORKELING | WATERFALLS

▬▬▬ Even if you're not a surfer, there are many ways to have aquatic adventures on Península de Nicoya. Snorkeling and scuba diving enthusiasts will find some of Costa Rica's clearest waters. If you're tired of the beach, hike along slippery rainforest trails that lead to waterfalls perfect for swimming.

JOAN VENDRELL/SHUTTERSTOCK ©

🗺 How To

Getting here Tours to Tortuga Island and the Chora Island Reserve often offer transportation options between your hotel and the point of departure. Montezuma is accessible by tours but most visitors rent a 4WD vehicle and drive there. It's an hour drive from Santa Teresa.

When to go Underwater visibility is best during dry season (December through April) when there is little rainfall. Much of the marine wildlife may also leave the area during the rainy season.

CARVERMOSTARDI/ALAMY STOCK PHOTO ©

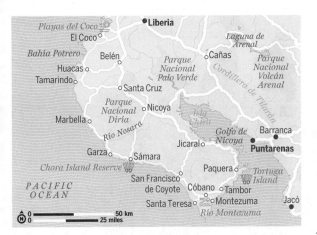

Top left Tortuga Island **Bottom left** Las Cataratas de Montezuma

Tortuga Island Off the southern coast of Península de Nicoya, this island is a popular snorkeling and scuba diving destination. It's only accessible by boat tours, which leave from Montezuma, Paquera and Santa Teresa, as well as from Jacó on the central Pacific coast. It's a 20-minute boat ride from Paquera, so travelers can do half-day tours specifically to experience the island's notable snorkeling sights. Tours from Montezuma take 45 minutes to arrive on the island and usually stay the full day to allow time for snorkeling or a scuba dive. Tortuga Island is part of the Islas Negritos Biological Reserve and the Tempisque Conservation Area.

Chora Island Reserve This small island near Sámara is perfect for a half-day snorkeling and kayaking tour. It's a 45-minute paddle via kayak to the island, where you can spend some time snorkeling or lying on the white-sand beaches. This island and the surrounding waters are home to rich purple, red and pink coral reefs and numerous schools of tropical fish. Day tours can be booked from Nosara and Punta Islita.

Río Montezuma Water adventures can happen in rivers too. Travelers descend on Montezuma to spend hours swimming in its three cascading waterfalls, **Las Cataratas de Montezuma**. Show off for Instagram: grab the Tarzan swing and fly through the jungle before plunging into the top waterfall.

〰️ Playas del Coco

For those staying in Guanacaste, Playas del Coco is a jump-off point for a morning of snorkeling or a full-day scuba tour. Boats will take you beyond the bay into the **Golfo de Papagayo** to swim with turtles, rays, spinyfish and other tropical water residents. Scuba divers will see an underwater world shaped by volcanic activity. There are a variety of small beaches around the gulf where your captain can stop for a beach snack or *cerveza*.

Most scuba and snorkel shops in Playas del Coco have offices on the main road or the beach to make an appointment.

34

Surf's
UP

SURFING | SWIMMING | BEACHES

Surfing is one of Costa Rica's biggest global attractions. Península de Nicoya has world-renowned waves, especially for expert surfers who want to ride with the best locals. Surfing is an institution in many of these Pacific coastal towns, and each has its own character.

🗺 How To

Getting here/around
Rent a 4WD that has space for your bags and your surfboard. The roads around many of these coastal towns are unpaved, so a 4WD is a necessity.

When to go Dry season (December through March) is best because the offshores are frequent for beginner surfers. Dry season is more crowded and the roads are dustier. Some of the best surfing beaches are inaccessible during the rainy season because of flooding.

Surf Smorgasbord

Surfers have a smorgasbord of breaks and beaches to choose from throughout Península de Nicoya. Each of these surf-centric coastal towns has a distinct vibe offering something different for every sort of traveler. All-inclusive surf camps are popular options in many of the areas that cater to beginner surfers. They offer multiday packages, including lessons, accommodations and meals. Expert surfers congregate in beach towns across the coast to show off their skills and teach tourists. Even though the dry season has ideal weather (sunny days, little rain), the water is colder and surfers will need a wetsuit.

🖊 Expert Surfers Only

Advanced surfers near Tamarindo head south to **Playa Langosta**. It's a more secluded beach known for consistent, challenging waves that test even veteran surfers. The most experienced surfers near Santa Teresa head to **Mal País/Punta Barigona**, especially when the Pacific Ocean is active.

Top left Playa Hermosa (p171) **Top right** Playa Langosta **Bottom left** Mal País

PENÍNSULA DE NICOYA EXPERIENCES

Nosara

Nosara has a multitude of perfect beaches for surfers of all levels. It may not have the same amount of traffic as other surf towns in the peninsula, but surfers like Nosara because the waves are consistent. **Playa Guiones** is known to be beginner-friendly and most surf schools are set up here. **Playa Nosara**, which has both a beach break and a reef break, is where more experienced surfers go for powerful waves.

Sámara

Sámara's beaches are known more for swimming than surfing. Absolute beginners will be comfortable here as the water is shallow, the waves are small and the bottom is sandy. This is where you learn the basics like practicing how to stand up on a surfboard and riding the white water to shore. A reef along the coast protects the bay from major waves, making it ideal for first-timers, other surfing newbies, and families with small children and elders.

Surfers & Sea Turtles

Two of Península de Nicoya's best surfing beaches are also the homes of nesting sea turtles. **Playa Ostional** is best known for the *arriba-das* when thousands of sea turtles hatch their eggs all at once, but it's also known for its strong waves among surfers in Nosara. The best surf season is January and February when its low season for the native olive ridley sea turtles. **Playa Grande**, near Tamarindo, brings surfers of all levels to its shores. It's less crowded than Tamarindo and has consistent waves. The beaches close at 6pm because Playa Grande is also the most important nesting site for leatherback turtles.

Left Playa Hermosa **Below** Tamarindo

Tamarindo

Tamarindo draws domestic and international travelers who want to surf hard and party harder. It's a great choice for beginner surfers because there are tons of breaks offering endless waves, and thus chances to practice. The waves break gently and the shore is all sand, which makes for soft landings. There are a host of surf camps and surf schools. Some offer daily lessons for a few hours, but for dedicated surfing students, many surf camps offer one-week packages with daily classes and individualized feedback to help you improve your stance and timing. One drawback of Tamarindo's geography is that the waves are tide dependent, so you may spend most of your day waiting for the waves to show up.

Santa Teresa

Adventurous surfers, digital nomads and aspiring healers have found a home in Santa Teresa, one of the most beloved beaches on Península de Nicoya. The currents that make most of the beaches terrible for swimming make them incredible for surfers. **Playa Hermosa** is best for beginners and **Playa Santa Teresa** is where most surf camps are located. Hardcore surfers hit nearby **Mal País** and **Playa Carmen** for serious swells.

35

Beach
VIBES

WATER | SUNBATHING | SWIMMING

Everyone comes to Costa Rica for its spectacular beaches. Península de Nicoya offers an entire coast of stunning sunsets and sunbathing spots under palm trees. Beachcombers can visit secluded beaches, or party hard on the sand and in the surf.

How To

Getting here/around
Having a rental car with 4WD will allow you to beach hop and explore the diverse beaches along the coast. Many roads are unpaved and taxi service is minimal and expensive.

When to go Visit January through April for the sunniest days with the least rain. But if you enjoy swimming under a warm drizzle, May through August usually yields sunny mornings and afternoon showers, with less crowds.

Península de Nicoya has a seemingly infinite number of beautiful beaches for all sorts of travelers. One could spend weeks driving along the coast, exploring a different beach town and stretch of Pacific coast each day. While surfing gets most of the attention, this coast is also perfect for lounging under palm trees or taking in the sun.

Playa Conchal

A stand-out beach on the northern part of the peninsula, Playa Conchal gets its name from its sprawling beaches, with white sand naturally made from seashells (*conchal* means shell in Spanish). A few larger hotel chains like Westin and the W have some fabulous luxury hotels along this beach. The shore is public, so you will find a mix of Tico families and international visitors. The water is crystal blue with a strong current, so watch small children by the shore.

(i) Coastal Alcoves

Visit **Playa Grande**, next to Tamarindo, for ecotourism adventures and quiet beaches. Much of the coast is prime turtle-hatching territory, but at the northern end of the beach, a trail leads to smaller, untouched beaches ideal for bathing and even snorkeling. Take a stroll to **Playa Ventanas** and **Playa Carbon**.

Top left Playa Santa Teresa (p175)
Top right Playa Conchal **Bottom left** Sámara (p175)

Nosara

While Nosara attracts surfers looking to build their skills, sunbathers and swimmers also have an abundance of options. The most popular beach in town is **Playa Guinoes**, but if you want a more secluded and lazy beach day with fewer people, visit **Playa Pelada**. There are many places there to lie in the sand, soak in tide pools and look at seashells. Sunset horseback riding is one of the most memorable excursions in Nosara. To add to the peaceful vibes here, there are numerous **yoga studios** and schools, thus attracting travelers who are interested in health and wellness.

Playa Junquillal

This charming and less-traveled beach town is perfect for a day trip when staying in Flamingo or Tamarindo. There are numerous coves to explore and pools for frolicking during low tide. Playa Junquillal's coastline lends itself to long, leisurely walks. **Sea**

♨ Nature's Hot Tubs

Take a break from the beaches and spend a few hours soaking in the **Malpaís tide pools**, also known as the Mar Azul tide pools. These mini 'hot tub' pools, south of Santa Teresa, are carved naturally into the rock formations and are among the best places on Península de Nicoya to watch the sunset. Pack some reef-safe sunscreen, a hat and even long sleeves if planning to stay awhile because there isn't much shade and the sun can be fierce. Water shoes are a safe bet to navigate the rocky terrain. Also bring water to stay hydrated.

Left Malpaís tide pools Below Sámara

turtles are part of the beach community here, and locals patrol the beaches at night to protect them and keep away poachers. The turtles are most active nesting and hatching between July and February.

Santa Teresa

Beautiful people gather at **Playa Santa Teresa** to watch surfers, walk their dogs and enjoy the sun with friends. Even though there's so much to see, it's easy to lose time staring at the miles of glittering tan sand, turquoise waters and the endless Pacific horizon.

Sámara

This stretch of the Pacific coast has some of the most swimmable beaches in Costa Rica. The coral reef that sits along the coast guards against the high waves and strong currents that surfers crave. Sámara and nearby Playa Buena Vista are a family-travel favorite because of their shallow water and smooth waves. This gentle and calm water is ideal for swimming and water activities such as paddleboarding, fishing, snorkeling and catamaran tours.

Protecting Costa Rica's Sea Turtles

GUARDING SEA TURTLES FROM OURSELVES

Sea turtles are the superstars of Península de Nicoya. The coast is home to thousands of endangered turtles who nest and hatch their eggs on the shores all year long. Conservation efforts are intertwined with Costa Rica's ecotourism initiatives and tourists play an important role in preserving the delicate environment.

Top left Leatherback turtle **Top center** Turtle nesting, Playa Ostional **Top right** Collecting olive ridley sea turtle eggs, Playa Ostional

STEPHANIE ROUSSEAU/SHUTTERSTOCK ©

One of the biggest draws to visiting Costa Rica is its captivating natural environment. Tourists quickly understand that humans are only a miniscule piece of the ecosystem because nature here is confronting and immersive. Most of the country's popular destinations require visitors to connect with the flora, fauna and weather. It's part of what makes Costa Rica magical.

Península de Nicoya is one of those locations where you have to slow down and recognize how nature is moving all around you. It's especially evident when it comes to sea turtles, a fixture along this coastline. Because endangered leatherback turtles nest here, and olive ridleys come in their thousands, Península de Nicoya has become a leader in global turtle conservation and ecotourism.

Leatherback turtles, typically found in Parque Nacional Marino Las Baulas, are the largest species of sea turtles, while olive ridleys, who take over Playa Ostional, are the smallest. One theory speculates that olive ridleys decide to hatch en masse to give themselves a better chance of surviving predators – a 'safety in numbers' plan of action. Even so, scientists have noted that both of these populations are dwindling over time, and the leatherback, in particular, is facing a serious threat of extinction. Both species are threatened by the poaching and selling of their eggs. These eggs are delicacies and are considered in many communities to have aphrodisiac powers. Another culprit for low survival rates is turtles getting caught up in commercial fishing nets or choking on plastic ocean pollution.

The role that conservation efforts will continue to have in sea turtle prospects cannot be downplayed. Volunteer opportunities have become more plentiful to help local conservationists conduct research on nesting ecology, population numbers, hatching success and the ratio of female to male turtles. Organizations are also committed to protecting turtle habitats. Most volunteers visiting from other countries stay a week or two. They help with a variety of tasks, including nighttime beach patrol, beach clean-ups and making signs. Some two-week volunteer programs are more in-depth, teaching visitors how to measure massive leatherbacks, and to tag and collect their eggs. Volunteers who support with data collection and monitor the beaches help ensure that the scientists' work can continue. Often volunteers will live at local homestays near the beach for the duration of their assignment. As with any volunteering opportunity, it's important that you research the credentials of any organization before signing up.

> Península de Nicoya is one of those locations where you have to slow down and recognize how nature is moving all around you.

Because so many tourists are drawn to Costa Rica's remarkable natural environment, it's important that everyone does their part even if not volunteering. For example, pick up trash on the beaches, even if it's not yours. And make sure you know the local hatching season so that you're not stepping on turtle eggs during a sunset stroll.

ⓘ Hatching Facts

Ostional is the only beach where poaching eggs is legal. The government allows locals to harvest eggs during the first three nights of an *arribada* (mass egg laying) because eggs laid on the first night often get destroyed by turtles on following nights.

During the two weeks that represent the middle of the egg's incubation period, the sand temperature in the nest determines the sex of the turtles that are hatched. If the sand temperature is above 30°C (86°F), the turtles will be female. If the temperature is below 27°C (81°F), the turtles will be male. In-between temperatures result in a mix.

SEEK OUT
These Sights

01 Leatherback sea turtles
The largest species of sea turtle nests and hatches on Península de Nicoya.

02 Surfboard
The allure of surfing permeates every beach along Península de Nicoya. Anyone can be surfer for a day.

03 Olive ridley sea turtles
Thousands of these tiny turtles spend days nesting and hatching on the shores.

04 ATV
All-terrain vehicles might look apocalyptic, but they're a convenient way to navigate dusty, dry-season roads in the southern Península de Nicoya.

05 Coyol
A common sight at roadside stands along the highways. Those recycled plastic soda bottles are full of homemade fermented liquor made from coyol palm tree sap.

06 White-faced monkeys
These adorable monkeys travel in packs and will steal your food. After years of tourists feeding them in exchange for photos, they will ransack your bag if you leave it unattended.

07 Yoga mat
Nosara and Santa Teresa attract budding instructors and health-conscious yoga enthusiasts on wellness retreats.

08 Coral
Gorgeous and colorful coral reefs offer epic snorkeling and scuba sights for underwater explorers.

09 Waterfalls
While Montezuma is the main attraction, there's plenty of smaller hidden waterfalls for swimming or wading.

10 Bikinis
Bikini shops are ubiquitous. Local designers create styles specifically for surfing while others are made solely for lounging and looking cute.

11 Kayaks
The transportation of choice for bioluminescent night tours, meandering through mangroves and accessing remote snorkeling adventures.

Listings

BEST OF THE REST

Surf Camps

Witch's Rock

Witch's Rock in Tamarindo caters to complete surfing newbies, as well as intermediate and advanced surfers who want to explore the more intense waves across Guanacaste.

Hostel La Posada

This seven-day surf camp in Santa Teresa combines five surf lessons with three yoga classes and professional sports massage. The hostel has private rooms with private bathrooms, and dormitory-style rooms.

Safari Surf School

The Safari Surf School in Nosara offers one-week all-inclusive stays with daily surf and yoga classes. The camp is led by a professional surfer and the suites have wi-fi, air-con and other amenities.

Peaks 'n Swells

This kid-friendly surf camp in Montezuma is geared toward families who want to learn how to surf together. Only three families are on-site at once, which gives individualized attention.

Mamawata's Women's Surf Retreat

This women-only surf camp in Nosara offers all-inclusive one-week retreats for solo travelers or small groups. The three retreats have different styles, but are all designed for maximum relaxation.

Restaurants

Pacifico Azul $$$

Get your fresh seafood fix at this restaurant on Playa Guiones in Nosara. The chefs offer family recipes cooked with local ingredients. Vegetarian and gluten-free options are available.

ChoroTacos $

Delicious tacos for meat-eaters, pescatarians and vegans at this small taqueria in the 'Pueblito Sur' plaza in Playas del Coco. Wash down the tacos, nachos and quesadillas with housemade *agua frescas*.

La Cevicheria $$

This busy yet unassuming restaurant on the main road through Santa Teresa sells ceviche in all the ways. Try Peruvian with *aje chile* sauce, or the Tropical with mango and ginger.

Ylang Ylang Restaurant $$$

Seafood and sushi dominate the menu at this beautiful beachside restaurant in Montezuma. Wide selection of meals to accommodate all tastes and dietary needs.

Rosi's Soda Tica $

Delicious and affordable hearty *casados* are served up at this Nosara *soda* (small local restaurants), which attracts locals and visitors. Visit one of the two locations by Playa Guiones.

La Doña Pizzeria $$

Wood-fired pizza and infinite Italian specialties are on the menu at this cozy restaurant in Malpaís. The chefs serve up an extensive selection with the freshest local ingredients.

Roots Bakery & Cafe $$

Choose from an array of tasty baked treats to appease your sweet tooth. Pick up breakfast, cinnamon rolls and organic coffee on your way to Playa Sámara.

B&Bs

Boho Lodge Montezuma I&I

This remote ecolodge located 5km from the Montezuma Falls has four air-conditioned units with kitchen and patios, as well as an outdoor pool and solid wi-fi.

Hotel Green Sanctuary Surf, Yoga & Spa

This family-owned and -operated boutique hotel is Costa Rica's first to be built entirely of shipping containers. Yogis frequent this sustainably designed space located in Nosara.

 Shopping

Papaya con Leche

Stop by Papaya con Leche, a sleek boutique in Tamarindo with locally designed women's wear for day and night. It specializes in custom-fit swimsuits and in-house handcrafted shoes.

Tica Surf Bikinis

Get a bikini designed for surfing. Since 2004, Tica owner and designer Veronica Quiros has been outfitting women surfers in Santa Teresa so they can focus on their sport and not their suit.

EK Art Jewelry

This store in Tamarindo is owned by a married couple of silversmiths, who sell gorgeous jewelry inspired by the natural sights of Costa Rica. One of a kind, wearable art.

Feria Organica

This local farmers' market takes place in Montezuma every Saturday from 10am to 2pm. Get fresh produce, baked goods, handmade soap, and even jewelry and fine art.

Bri'ah Art Gallery

Get a keepsake piece made by local artists at this gallery of modern art in Santa Teresa. It also offers painting parties for families and ones with wine for adults.

 Tours

Carrillo Tours

For nature adventures near Playa Sámara, book a tour with Carillo Tours. It is Costa Rican–owned and offer shuttles, sea/mangrove kayak tours, horseback riding, and visits to natural reserves.

Xplore Costa Rica

Xplore Costa Rica leads various nature tours throughout the Tamarindo area. Travelers can choose from ziplining, river rafting, sunset catamaran tours and various adventures.

Ecological Association Paquera, Lepanto & Cóbano (ASEPALECO)

This conservation group runs tours of the Karen Mogensen Reserve which is a privately-owned sanctuary for local wildlife species and to protect the rivers and natural springs.

Nicoya Surf & SUP

Sign up with these local experts for surf lessons or SUP (stand-up paddleboarding) in Santa Teresa, Playa Hermosa and Montezuma. Beginners and intermediates will enjoy some of the region's best waves.

Zuma Tours

Zuma Tours has been in business for 30 years in the Montezuma and Santa Teresa area. It offers various tours on land and sea, including scuba diving, sportfishing and ATVing.

 Scan to find more things to do in Península de Nicoya online

CENTRAL PACIFIC COAST

BEACHES | MARINE SPORTS | NATIONAL PARKS

Experience
the Central
Pacific
Coast online

Observe bountiful bird species at **Parque Nacional Carara** (p193)
🚗 25min from Jacó

Parque Nacional Carara

Tárcoles

Bijagual

Río Grande de Condelaria

Golfo de Nicoya

Río Pirris

Step up your surfing skills in **Playa Jacó** (p201)
🚗 2hr from San José

Jacó

Valle de Parrita

Parrita

Cheer on the brave surfers competing weekly in **Playa Hermosa** (p201)
🚗 15min from Jacó

Cruise along the coast of **Bahía Biesanz** on a catamaran (p191)
⛴ 30min from Manuel Antonio

CENTRAL PACIFIC COAST
Trip Builder

PACIFIC OCEAN

▬▬▬ The central Pacific coast is one of Costa Rica's biggest tourist destinations because of its proximity to San José and its abundance of mind-blowing beaches and ecotourism adventures. Visitors can relax, party, dive and hike through stunning nature scenes.

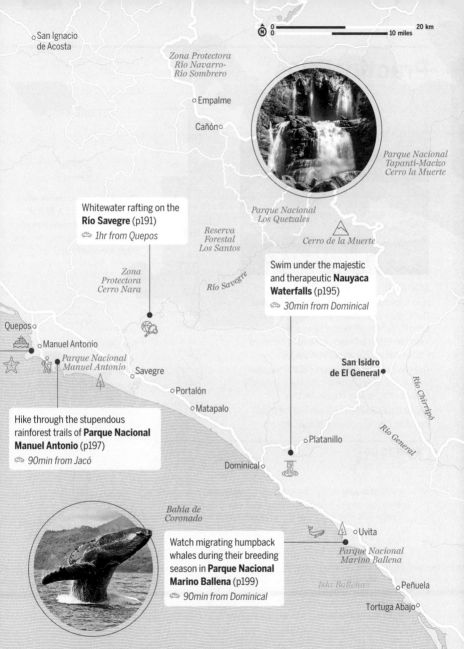

San Ignacio
de Acosta

Zona Protectora
Río Navarro-
Río Sombrero

Empalme

Cañón

Parque Nacional
Tapantí-Macizo
Cerro la Muerte

Whitewater rafting on the Río Savegre (p191)
🚗 1hr from Quepos

Parque Nacional
Los Quetzales

Reserva
Forestal
Los Santos

Cerro de la Muerte

Swim under the majestic and therapeutic Nauyaca Waterfalls (p195)
🚗 30min from Dominical

Zona
Protectora
Cerro Nara

Río Savegre

Quepos

Manuel Antonio

Parque Nacional
Manuel Antonio

Savegre

San Isidro
de El General

Río Chirripó

Hike through the stupendous rainforest trails of Parque Nacional Manuel Antonio (p197)
🚗 90min from Jacó

Portalón

Matapalo

Platanillo

Río General

Dominical

Bahía de
Coronado

Watch migrating humpback whales during their breeding season in Parque Nacional Marino Ballena (p199)
🚗 90min from Dominical

Uvita

Parque Nacional
Marino Ballena

Isla Ballena

Peñuela

Tortuga Abajo

20 km

10 miles

Practicalities

ARRIVING

Juan Santamaría International Airport, San José (SJO) Most travelers will rent a car from SJO to drive to the Pacific coastal towns, or take a private shuttle to their hotel. Flights to Quepos, a hub along the central Pacific coast, are 25-minutes from San José.

Quepos La Managua Airport (XQP) This small airport only serves domestic travelers, especially those wanting to visit Manuel Antonio.

Public buses Routes to various coastal cities including Jacó, Quepos and Manuel Antonio.

HOW MUCH FOR A

Guaro sour
US$3

Craft beer
US$4

Smoothie
US$6

GETTING AROUND

Car Rentals give travelers more freedom to explore. A 4WD is ideal for unpaved roads en route to waterfalls, rainforest hikes and other eco-adventures.

Taxi Uber is available in Jacó, Quepos and Manuel Antonio. Most hotels or homeshares have local taxi drivers for hire. Renting a taxi and driver for the day is an option, particularly for tours.

WHEN TO GO

JAN–APR
Peak season; dry season is sunny with little rain

MAY–AUG
Less crowded; rainy season begins; sunny mornings, afternoon storms

SEP–OCT
Rainiest months and end of rainy season; flooding possible; some businesses close

NOV–DEC
Holiday season begins; storms subside

Bus Public buses are a cheaper option from San José, but are less comfortable and stop a lot. Once on the central Pacific coast, buses are a cost-effective way to visit beach towns that are close to each other.

EATING & DRINKING

The central Pacific coast offers a variety of typical Tico flavors. No breakfast in Costa Rica is complete without *gallo pinto* (pictured top right), the quintessential national dish of white rice and black beans. In honor of this region's party vibes, try all the *guaro* concoctions your stomach can stand. *Guaro,* made of sugar cane, is the national liquor; Cacique is the national brand. Chili *guaro* shots and *guaro* sours (picture bottom right) are most popular.

Best quirky ambience
El Avión (p207)

Must-try microbrews
Puddlefish Brewery (p206)

WHERE TO STAY

This region boasts a wide variety of beautiful coastal towns. Choose from locales near grand national parks or laid-back beach communities.

CONNECT & FIND YOUR WAY

Connect Wi-fi is generally available at most hotels, restaurants and homesharing properties. Cell service is solid in tourist-friendly areas along the coast. Cellular service may be unreliable or scattered on secluded roads where there's limited wi-fi access.

Navigation If planning to explore remote beaches or mountain areas, it's best to download maps before leaving wi-fi areas.

Town/Village	Pro/Con
Jacó	A plethora of activities and beaches close to the airport. Big party scene.
Manuel Antonio	Lush ecolodges and resorts. LGBTIQ+ friendly vibes. Can get crowded.
Dominical	A popular surfer destination known for its waves. Quirky beach town.
Uvita	Best spot for whale-watching. Far from the airport.

STAY AWARE

Jacó is a party town where many travelers come to indulge in drugs and sex tourism. Solo travelers should stay aware of their surroundings.

MONEY

ATMs are readily available and easily accessible in major tourist areas such as Jacó. Avoid paying credit-card transaction fees and taxes by paying for meals, groceries and souvenirs in cash.

36 The Great
OUTDOORS

TOURS | VIEWS | ADVENTURE SPORTS

███ Ecotourism excursions are at the heart of Costa Rica's tourism because there are so many awe-inspiring ways to connect with the country's vibrant natural environment. Fly through the jungle on a zipline, parasail above the rainforest or ride horses along the beach during sunset. There's enough high-octane activities and low-key experiences to appeal to every sort of traveler.

PHOTO COURTESY VISTA LOS SUEÑOS ADVENTURE PARK, JACO - COSTA RICA, VLSCR.COM ©

🗺 How To

Getting around Many nature-focused tours offer transport from your accommodations and include it in the cost of the tour. Renting a vehicle allows for more opportunities to explore the region. Public buses run regularly along the coast and to more inland towns, but may require changing buses in Quepos.

When to go Rain can affect the safety of many outdoor activities, so it's best to visit in the dry season (December through April). It's also more crowded with international tourists.

RANCHO LA MERCED ©

Top left Vista Los Sueños Adventure Park **Bottom left** Rancho La Merced

Thrillseekers on the central Pacific coast can choose from a variety of adventure parks, which offer an assortment of activities, such as ziplining, ATV riding and canyoning (waterfall rappelling) all in one place.

Vista Los Sueños Adventure Park Near Jacó, this place serves up family-friendly excursions. It offers an extensive playground and is also known for the safety, quality and maintenance of its cables and equipment. For those who want to stay on solid ground, Vista Los Sueños offers chocolate tours as well as horseback-riding tours that explore waterfalls and wildlife. You can spend a full day here doing a combination of tours; there's also a delicious restaurant with Tico cuisine.

Zion Paragliding Paragliding is not for the faint of heart, but it awards fearless adventurers with a literal bird's-eye view of the Pacific coast. In Dominical, Zion is a paragliding school that provides tandem experiences as well as classes for those intent on learning how to fly. The tour takes brave visitors up to Cerro Escalares where you and your expert paragliding guide will take off (ie run off the mountain). The flight time is 15 to 20 minutes and offers astonishing views of the jungle, birds and beach below, where you'll land. Photos cost extra.

Rancho La Merced If you're closer to Uvita, this ranch provides horseback-riding tours to nearby waterfalls during the day and to Playa Hermosa for sunset. Because Rancho La Merced is an actual working cattle ranch, there's also a unique Cowboy Experience, where you spend a few hours herding cattle, learning how to check cows and calves in the grass, and other typical daily ranch tasks.

El Miro

Go to **Miro Mountain** for the best Pacific coast views in Jacó. It's located in the southern part of Jacó. Once you climb the mountain path, there's a lookout with grand views of the coast. To the left, you'll see an abandoned hotel in the distance. As you descend, you can stop at the building to see walls covered in animal murals. Further down, you'll see numerous types of trees, as well as monkeys, scarlet macaws, toucans, wild turkeys and sloths. There's also a variety of small animals, such as spiders and leaf-cutter ants.

■ **By Wilson Viviano,** owner of Hostel de Haan in Jacó

37 Aquatic ADVENTURE

DIVING | SAILING | SNORKELING

▬▬▬ Nurture your inner mermaid in the enchanting waters of the central Pacific coast. This region boasts some of the country's best scuba diving locales plus top-notch snorkeling in out-of-way coastal coves. The marine aspects of the national parks in this region are just as magical as the land. Stand-up paddleboarding, banana boats and catamaran cruises are all available, too.

OGPHOTO/GETTY IMAGES ©

🗺 How To

Getting around Most tour operators in this area include transportation in their prices. If you're staying in one area and plan to do several tours, you probably won't need a rental car. Public buses make stops along Ruta 34, but you'll need a taxi or other transport from the bus stop to your lodging.

When to go Dry season is ideal for enjoying all of the water adventures. Rainy season means more cancelled excursions.

Tip Visit sinac.go.cr before visiting national parks to book tickets and confirm hours.

JORGE A. RUSSELL/SHUTTERSTOCK ©

Top left Parque Nacional Marino Ballena **Bottom left** Adapted stand-up paddleboarding (SUP) class, Playa Herradura

Parque Nacional Marino Ballena National parks have some of the best places to enjoy the ocean, whether swimming in it or sailing on it. This park is one of the best areas for scuba diving in Costa Rica. The park protects the largest coral reef in Central America, and there are more than 80 marine species living in its waters. It's become a destination for scuba divers because of the thriving underwater ecosystem.

Parque Nacional Manuel Antonio Snorkeling fans can experience some of the best visibility and biodiversity off the coast of this park. While you can bring our own snorkeling gear to the beach, it's best to book a guided snorkeling tour where you can kayak away from the shore into deeper waters.

Bahía Biesanz Many tours come here, where the water is clear and still, offering ideal conditions for snorkeling, kayaking and paddleboarding. Catamaran cruises are a trendy, and sometimes boozy, way to visit this beach for snorkeling and sunsets. Enjoy stunning views of the central Pacific coastline and make new friends as you sail along the glimmering bay.

Playa Herradura Near Jacó, this beach is excellent for beginner divers and those taking certification courses, even though there's not the same level of rare marine wildlife. Instead it's a more popular port for sportfishing because of its year-round gamefish such as tuna and marlin. Herradura's calm waters also make it a fun beach to take stand-up paddleboarding (SUP) classes.

ⓘ Whitewater Rafting

Much of the water-centric excursions focus on beaches or waterfalls. However, whitewater rafting excursions on the **Río Savegre** are an action-packed day trip for travelers staying on the coast. Rafting trips traverse the Río Savegre, one of Costa Rica's cleanest and most stunning rivers, which is only a one-hour drive from Quepos. The full-day tour usually includes transportation and meals. You're in the river for two hours navigating exciting stretches of Class II and Class III rapids, with pit stops at hidden waterfalls and swimming holes. A safety kayaker is with the group at all times.

38 Sloths, Crocs & **TOUCANS**

HIKING | NATIONAL PARKS | WILDLIFE

▬▬▬ A visit to Costa Rica isn't complete without seeing a sloth or a toucan. National parks established by the government and private reserves safeguard one of the country's most precious resources: its flora and fauna. These parks offer the opportunity to encounter Costa Rica's other resident creatures too, such as crocodiles, monkeys, macaws, iguanas and motmots.

GIANFRANCO VIVI/SHUTTERSTOCK ©

🗺 How To

Getting around You'll need a car for all of the excursions listed, and a 4WD to visit Los Campesinos Reserve. If you have a private shuttle, ask the driver to stop at the Crocodile Bridge. It's on the way!

When to go Outside September and October – when flooding may cancel outdoor activities – any time of year is OK. The driest and sunniest weather is from December through April.

Guides When possible, hire a guide. They're trained to point out the wildlife you might miss.

ARTUSH/SHUTTERSTOCK ©

Parque Nacional Carara Birdwatchers love this national park. It has a special ecosystem where tropical dry rainforest and tropical rainforest merge and overlap. Plants native to both ecosystems grow here attracting countless species of insects and thus copious amounts of hungry birds. Carara, a 25-minute drive north of Jacó, was established in 1998 and covers 51 sq km of land protecting the Río Tarcoles basin. It's full of various short 1km to 2km trails and an accessible trail for visitors with a disability. Not only is it smoothly paved for wheelchairs, there are also braille signs and statues of the local birds.

'Crocodile Bridge' Also near Jacó is this famous bridge on Ruta 34, the Costanera Sur Hwy. Tourists will park along either side of the road to walk this bridge, which overlooks the Río Tarcoles, said to have the largest number of crocodiles in the world. The bridge is part of the main route travelers take from Jacó down the coast to Dominical and Uvita. Now there are restaurants and souvenir shops catering to tourists who come there just to walk the bridge and gaze down on dozens of crocodiles.

Los Campesinos Reserve An hour's drive from Quepos, this reserve is a rural ecotourism experience. On private property owned by local Ticos, visitors can hike through primary and secondary rainforest on a suspension bridge while naturalist guides point out all of the native flora and fauna.

Top left 'Crocodile Bridge' **Bottom left** Yellow-throated toucan

ⓘ Footwear & Guides

Pack a pair of hiking shoes or closed-toe hiking sandals if you plan to visit any national parks or nature reserves. Having a good grip on the trails and foot protection from wildlife is a necessity.

Always hire a guide when visiting the parks and refuges to see the wildlife. It's a wonderful way to get to know locals, and to maximize the experience. Not only can they see camouflaging animals and plant life, they also can point out wildlife you never even knew existed. Without a guide, you miss out on a lot of jungle surprises.

39 Cascading CATARATAS

WATERFALLS | HIKING | SWIMMING

▬▬ Waterfall excursions are ubiquitous across Costa Rica, and the falls themselves are veritable Instagram celebrities. You could fill a vacation doing nothing but visiting waterfalls around the central Pacific coast. There are well-maintained falls specifically for tourist excursions, but also more rustic, less-visited options for those prepared to work to reach them.

SESTOVIC/GETTY IMAGES ©

🗺 How To

Getting around A 4WD ensures you can handle any river crossings or other unpaved and unpredictable terrain.

When to go More rain means robust waterfalls. Too much rain means flooded roads and canceled excursions.

September and October, the rainiest months, are worst for waterfall hikes. December is great – it's the beginning of dry season, yet the rivers are still full from rainy season.

Gear Wear water shoes with good grip, and consider bringing a dry bag.

COLIN D. YOUNG/SHUTTERSTOCK ©

Top left Nauyaca Waterfalls **Bottom left** Catarata Manantial de Agua Viva

Nauyaca Waterfalls These falls are among the most majestic waterfall experiences in the region. They're only a 20-minute drive into the mountains from Dominical. Visitors can choose to walk 1.2km to the falls or take a horseback ride through the rainforest. The hike consists of a 2km trek from the parking area to the trail, and then another 4km to reach the falls. It's a mix of smooth and unpaved paths with a few manageable ascents and takes about one hour to 90 minutes each way. You'll eventually arrive at two intoxicating falls, upper and lower, with stairs leading to each one. These waterfalls, measuring a combined 61m high, tower over a spacious pool of deep blue water, which is perfect for swimming after the long hike. There are even bathrooms and changing facilities before the steps.

Catarata Bijagual The imposing Catarata Bijagual is a 40-minute drive from Jacó and is one of the most remarkable sights in the area. At 183m high, it's one of the tallest waterfalls in Costa Rica. The entry for hikers is US$20, but as with Nauyaca many visitors take a horseback riding tour to the falls. The hiking trail has several steep ascents and is moderately challenging. It should be avoided during and after rain. You're rewarded with some sweet swimming pools once you get to the enthralling waterfall.

🪣 Waterfall Wonderland

A family-friendly waterfall adventure, **Catarata Uvita** is 10 minutes from Uvita by car. A portion of the trail to the waterfall is paved, leading to the first swimming hole. Walk through the river to play in the waterfall. There's a naturally occurring waterslide carved in the rocks.

For an ecotourism excursion with nature hikes and waterfalls, visit **Santa Lucia Falls**. Two Tico brothers own the land and offer guided tours through the jungle to three waterfalls. It's a 30-minute drive from Dominical.

A 10-minute drive from Jacó, **Las Monas Rainforest** has eight different waterfalls. A local guide will identify the best waterfalls for swimming and safety.

40 Pure NATURE

ADVENTURE | WILDLIFE | HIKING

Costa Rica's national parks are global treasures and visiting them is magical. It's hard to overstate the majesty and magnitude of nature, uninterrupted and in its purest forms. Experience the grandeur of the biodiversity here.

SIMON DANNHAUER/SHUTTERSTOCK ©

🗺 How To

Getting here/around
While renting a car brings freedom of movement, public buses leave from downtown San José to Jacó almost hourly on the weekends, and multiple times a day during the week. Private shuttles should be arranged before arrival.

When to go December through April (dry season) is sunny, gorgeous and crowded. There are sunny days, afternoon storms and less crowds during May, July and August.

Tickets Entry to Parque Nacional Manuel Antonio is US$18. Entry to Parque Nacional Marino Ballena is US$6.

IMAGEBROKER.COM/SHUTTERSTOCK ©

Visiting the national parks is a uniquely Costa Rican experience. It immerses the traveler physically in its robust natural ecosystems, and immerses us spiritually in the culture of the country.

Parque Nacional Manuel Antonio

Although one of the country's most visited national parks, Parque Nacional Manuel Antonio is also its smallest. It was established in 1972 and spans 1950 hectares of land and 55,000 marine hectares, which include coral reefs. It packs a lot of biodiversity into a compact space. Its beaches are spectacular and wildlife is abundant. Visitors can hike with experienced naturalist guides to search for sloths, toucans, multiple species of monkeys and even adorable, colorful little crabs.

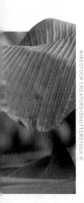

WIRESTOCK CREATORS/SHUTTERSTOCK ©

ⓘ The Whale's Tail

Make sure to check the tide chart before venturing out to the Whale's Tail. It's best to visit during low tide when the shore and rock formations are exposed and you can easily walk along it. It's a great place to snorkel during low tides, so bring your mask (fins are prohibited).

Top left Parque Nacional Manuel Antonio **Top right** Rainbow crab, Parque Nacional Manuel Antonio **Bottom left** Red-backed squirrel monkey, Parque Nacional Manuel Antonio

One of the highlights is **Playa Manuel Antonio**, a crescent-shaped white-sand beach bordering verdant rainforest. Also make sure to hike to **Cathedral Point**, a short 1.2km trail with lots of stairs. The steep change in elevation opens up impressive views of the Pacific coast.

Tickets are required to enter the park and can be purchased online. You'll need your passport number to complete the reservation. It's smart to book your visit in advance, especially during high/dry season and on weekends. For self-guided tours, purchase tickets on SINAC's website (sinac.go.cr). A guided tour is often more rewarding if you want to look for wildlife because the guides' eyes are trained to find the camouflaged animals, and they know where to look. Guides also bring telescopes! Tickets are included in the price of guided tours, and the guide will have them. Manuel Antonio also has trails that are accessible for people in wheelchairs.

🚗 Arriving at Parque Nacional Manuel Antonio

The road to entering this park is one lane and winds up a mountain. Drive slowly for safety and exceptional views. There's no official parking area for the national park. Visitors can patronize the private parking areas available around the park entrance for a daily rate of US$7 to US$10. Be prepared for folks along the road selling overpriced tours and parking as you approach the entrance. Arrive early when the park opens for best parking options. Also, map your route and/or book a certified tour before you leave to eliminate uncertainty and get the best value.

FAR LEFT: STEFAN NEUMANN/SHUTTERSTOCK ©,
LEFT: CLAUDE HUOT/SHUTTERSTOCK ©

Left Whale's Tail **Below**
Humpback whale, Parque
Nacional Marino Ballena

Parque Nacional Marino Ballena

Located on the coast adjacent to Uvita, Parque
Nacional Marino Ballena was established in 1990
and protects 5510 hectares of beach, mangrove
estuary, lowland rainforest and marine habitats.
It's best known for the **Whale's Tail** (or Tómbolo),
a portion of the coastline that is shaped like a
whale's tail when viewed from the air. This appro-
priately named area is also the best place in Costa
Rica to look for humpback whales, who breed in
the waters here.

There are four different entrances to the park:
Uvita, Colonia, Ballena and Piñuela. The Uvita
sector, where the Whale's Tail is, and the Colonia
sector, where the surfers hang out, are the most
popular entrances. They are the easiest to access
regardless of the tide and weather, and are open
daily from 7am to 6pm. While there are hiking
trails, the beaches are the highlight. Besides the
Tómbolo, check out the other beautiful beaches:
Bahía, **Colonia**, **Ballena**, **Arco** and **Piñuelas**.
The peak season for watching humpback whales
is July to November, but dolphins swim here
year round.

41 Beaches & COVES

SWIMMING | SURFING | SUNBATHING

Postcard-worthy beaches line the central Pacific coast of Costa Rica. Beach lovers are spoiled for choice by the numerous coastal coves. Surfers, swimmers and sunbathers will be enthralled by the inviting turquoise waters and the expansive stretches of glimmering sand.

🗺️ How To

Getting around For travelers based in one beach town, private shuttles or public buses are a cost-effective and low-maintenance way to travel. Those who wish to hop between beaches should rent a car with 4WD to access unpaved roads.

When to go Dry season (December through April) has less rain but more tourists. It's rainforest, so some areas get year-round rain, though it's less frequent during the dry season. Some surfers prefer the massive waves during rainy season.

Surfing

The Pacific Ocean's waves are world renowned for both surfing aficionados and curious beginners. **Playa Jacó** attracts novices and experts because the surf varies with the tides: low tide creates ideal conditions for newbies, while high tide invites brave, seasoned surfers. **Playa Hermosa**, only 15 minutes south of Jacó, is where surf champions are made. It boasts some of the biggest waves in Costa Rica. Its intense breaks bring experienced surfers here weekly to show off in an open surf competition, happening every Saturday.

Although known to have some of the country's biggest waves, **Playa Dominical** is less visited than Jacó. Also, if you're visiting Parque Nacional Manuel Antonio, stop by **Playa Espadilla Sur** to surf some small waves during high tide. It is the main beach

📷 Sunset Performance

Catch the sunset. The Pacific coast sunsets are a theatrical performance. The sky is painted with brilliant shades of orange, pink and purple that melt together across the horizon. The sun sets every day in Costa Rica between 5:30pm and 6pm. Get to the beach by 5pm to catch the pyrotechnics.

Top left Playa Jacó **Top right** Playa Dominical **Bottom left** Playa Espadilla Sur

in Manuel Antonio, so it may be exceptionally crowded during high season. When visiting Uvita, **Playa Colonia** is where you can find the surfers hanging out and waves suited to beginners. Note that you'll have to pay the park's entrance fee to surf here.

Swimming & Sunworshipping

In this region, a lot of the most spectacular beaches are located near or within the national parks. **Playa Espadilla Norte**, just north of Parque Nacional Manuel Antonio, is a free public beach. There are tons of bars and restaurants nearby, so you can easily spend the whole day here. There are also various vendors renting chairs and umbrellas, or selling things like fresh coconuts or cold beers, so bring cash. **Playa Espadilla Sur** is more secluded and tranquil because it's contained within the national park, but you'll have to pay the US$18 entrance fee to visit.

〜 Safe Swimming

Costa Rica has no national lifeguard program, so most of the lifeguards you see at the beaches along the central Pacific coast are trained volunteers with a few from Cruz Roja (Red Cross). In response to numerous drownings in 2019 the government passed a law to create a National Lifeguard Corps, but nothing has been officially instituted. Major beaches like Jacó, Dominical, Manuel Antonio, Playa Hermosa in Uvita and Playa Ballena have volunteer teams, but most of the small beaches have no lifeguards. Do research before swimming at secluded beaches because of strong rip currents.

Tárcoles
Playa Mantas
Playa Blanca
Playa Jacó • Jacó
Valle de Parrita
Río Pirris
Reserva Forestal Los Santos
Cerro de la Muerte
Playa Hermosa
○ Parrita
Quepos
○ Manuel Antonio
San Isidro de El General ●
Playa Espadilla Norte
○ Savegre
Playa Espadilla Sur
○ Matapalo
PACIFIC OCEAN
Playa Dominical
○ Dominical
○ Uvita
Bahía de Coronado
Playa Colonia
Playa Ventanas
0 40 km
0 20 miles
Tortuga Abajo

Left Playa Jacó (p201) **Below** Playa Espadilla Sur

There's a variety of lesser-known beaches surrounding some of the popular tourist spots like Jacó and Uvita. **Playa Mantas**, a 15-minute drive north of Jacó, offers gentle waves for a relaxed and family-friendly experience. Its neighbor, **Playa Blanca** also embodies *pura vida* vibes. There are no waves on this section of the coast, making it a wonderful spot for wading but also for snorkeling and diving excursions. These beaches can get especially crowded with domestic tourists on weekends because it is so close to San José (about 90 minutes via highway).

A local favorite, **Playa Ventanas** is on the Costa Ballena near Uvita. It fringes a mesmerizing bay with deep azure water and long stretches of sand perfect for walking or frolicking. Tico families often come here for picnics and a fun game of *fútbol* (soccer). Don't miss the caves at the north end of the beach. During low tide you can walk through the first one, but make sure to be out by high tide.

THINGS THAT
Make You Go Ahhh...

01

02

03

04

01 Crocodiles
The stars of the world-renowned 'Crocodile Bridge' (p193), where tourists come to watch them swim and hunt in the Río Tarcoles.

02 Humpback whales
These majestic mammals breed along the Pacific coast. See them from mid-December though mid-April; brave rainy season to see them from July through November.

03 Ziplines
Flying above the jungle is one of the region's most beloved and adrenaline-pumping adventure excursions.

04 Howler monkeys
The loud monkeys that wake you up early in the morning. Their howls and bellows were used in the movie, *Jurassic Park*.

POSTCARD

FROM:

05 Waterfalls
One of the most common sights and excursions in the area for swimming, hikes, picnics and photos. Always breathtaking.

06 The Whale's Tail
The whale-tail-shaped shore in Parque Nacional Marino Ballena at Uvita (p199) is the home of humpback whales.

07 Leaf cutter ants
The hardest working insects in the jungle. They work steadily, carrying leaf bits back and forth across the rainforest.

08 SUP
If surfing is too intense, stand up paddle boards are an alternative way to enjoy time on the rivers and calm, coastal waters.

09 Fer-de-Lance snakes
One of the most dangerous snakes in Costa Rica. It's venomous and aggressive, and lives in the rainforest.

Listings

CENTRAL PACIFIC COAST REVIEWS

BEST OF THE REST

 **Bars & Nightlife**

Puddlefish Brewery $$

Hang out in Jacó at Puddlefish's outdoor beer garden and sample brews made on site. Stay for the live music most nights of the week.

Republik Lounge $$

Part nightclub, part hookah lounge. Ultimate Jacó pool-party spot, with VIP tables, multiple rooms and varying DJs.

Rum Bar $

Drop in to this spot if you're looking for live music and tasty cocktails in Dominical. A great place to watch sports and play pool, foozball and darts.

Orange Pub $

Popular nightlife spot for young locals and tourists in Jacó. The party doesn't get started until after 10pm and gets packed on weekends.

Uvita Beer Garden $$

Brews and tacos are plentiful at this beer garden. Dozens of local beers available along with international favorites.

Mosaic Wine Bar $$$

The extensive wine list and craft cocktails are a standout at this restaurant and bar in Uvita. Uses local ingredients. Awesome sushi menu.

Backyard Bar $

Arrive around 4pm for the spectacular weekly surf competition on Playa Hermosa. Stay for sunset, and party with locals and tourists into the night.

(i) Tours

Kayak Jacó

A reliable tour operator for snorkeling, kayaking and SUP adventures in Playa Agujas. Sixteen years of experience guiding tours.

Costa Rica Jade Tours

One of the best tour operators for Parque Nacional Manuel Antonio and mangrove tours of Damas Island. Knowledgeable, friendly and experienced guides.

Dolphin Tours

With 20 years of experience in responsible sea tourism, this company operates whale-watching boat tours from Uvita. It takes safety and sustainability seriously.

Adventure Tours

Over a decade of experience managing tours in Jacó and Manuel Antonio. It specializes in nature adventures like ATV tours, whitewater rafting and monkey tours.

Manuel Antonio Canopy Safari Zip Line

The oldest established canopy tour in the region. Besides ziplining, it includes rappelling lines, a suspension bridge and a wildlife sanctuary.

Bahía Adventures

For 20 years, this tour company has been committed to sustainable marine tourism in Uvita. It offers snorkeling and scuba diving excursions as well as whale-watching.

Pineapple Tours

Specializing in kayaking and SUP in Dominical. No experience needed to enjoy the mangrove tours.

Restaurants

Soda Jacó Rústico $

This local *soda* (small local restaurant) serving Costa Rican cuisine is known for hearty portions buffet-style at an affordable price. Laid-back vibes and consistent quality.

Indómitos Cafe $$

Copious healthy options for vegetarians and vegas in Uvita. Start your day with a superfruit smoothie or healthy craft concoction.

El Avión $$

This restored 1980s gun-running airplane was converted to a restaurant and cocktail bar 1.5km away from Playa Dominical. Try the cocktails and check out the cockpit views.

Gabriella's Steak Seafood & Pasta $$$

This open-air restaurant sits on the marina in Quepos. It's the perfect place to catch the sunset and feast on a delicious seafood dinner.

Tiki Bar $$$

Enjoy the vivid Pacific sunsets over seafood and cocktails at this hotel restaurant on Playa Jacó.

La Choza de Alejo $$

Authentic Mexican food on the Pacific coast of Costa Rica. A surprising gem in Uvita with yummy fresh fruit margaritas and good portions that bring back repeat customers.

Emilio's Cafe $$

Sweeping mountain views and some of the freshest seafood in Manuel Antonio. Enjoy friendly service, live music and immersive wildlife.

Cafe Mono Congo $$

Health-conscious eaters, vegetarians and vegans will rejoice at this breakfast and lunch eatery in Dominical along the Río Barú. Fresh and flavorful options abound for meat-lovers too.

Playa Jacó (p201)

Shopping

Dantica Gallery

The gallery located in the Jacó Walk Shopping Center sells art and home goods made by talented Tico artisans. Perfect for souvenir shopping for yourself and loved ones.

Villa Vanilla Spice Tour and Shop

Stock up on organic spices after a tour of a working organic biodynamic spice farm near Manuel Antonio. Bring home vanilla extract, Ceylon cinnamon and chocolates made on-site.

Mariposita Gift Shop and Gallery

This humble locally owned gift shop in Quepos is a wonderful place to purchase typical Costa Rican souvenirs and art created by local artisans. An assortment of wooden crafts and gorgeous paintings.

Scan to find more things to do in the Central Pacific Coast online

SOUTHERN COSTA RICA & PENÍNSULA DE OSA

ECOTOURISM | RAINFOREST | WILDLIFE

Experience
Southern
Costa Rica
& Península
de Osa
online

Watch quetzals in the highlands of **Providencia de Dota** (p212)

🚗 2hr drive from San José

Summit **Cerro Chirripó**, Costa Rica's highest peak (p214)

🚗 2hr drive from Providencia

See pre-Colombian spheres at El Sitio **Museo Finca 6** (p219)

🚗 2hr drive from Cerro Chirripó

Dive deep and explore coral reefs at **Isla del Caño** (p218)

⛵ 45min boat ride from Bahía Drake

Hike La Leona coastal trail at **Parque Nacional Corcovado** (p224)

🚗 2hr drive from Puerto Jiménez

Providencia de Dota
Ojo del Agua
San Gerardo de Dota
Parque Nacional Chirripó
División
Parque Nacional Canaán
Los Quetzales
Savegre
Cerro Chirripó
Rivas
Portalón
● San Isidro de El General
Matapalo
Platanillo
Dominical
Escalares
Parque Nacional Marino Ballena
Uvita
Río General
Isla Ballena
Peñuela
Tortuga Abajo
Bahía de Coronado
Palmar Sur
Palmar Norte
Sierpe
Chacarita
Reserva Forestal Golfo Dulce
Isla del Caño
Bahía Drake
Drake
Parque Nacional Piedras Blancas
Río Claro
Agujitas
Rincón
Rancho
La Palma
Neily
Quemado
Golfo Dulce
Parque Nacional Corcovado
Puerto Jiménez
Laguna Corcovado
Península de Osa
PACIFIC OCEAN
Carate
Matapalo

SOUTHERN COSTA RICA & PENÍNSULA DE OSA
Trip Builder

▬▬▬▬ This region boasts unmatched biodiversity and some of the most unique ecotourism and cultural tourism experiences in the country. Amid the highlands, cloud forests, indigenous communities and pristine rainforests, travelers can have extraordinary adventures that are distinctly Costa Rican.

🧭 0 —————— 50 km
0 —————— 25 miles

Practicalities

ARRIVING

Juan Santamaria International Airport (SJO) From the airport in Alajuela it's a two-hour drive to Providencia de Dota. Bahía Drake and Puerto Jiménez have domestic airports with daily flights from SJO.

CONNECT

Wi-fi is minimal and cell service spotty in Providencia de Dota and Terraba. Download navigation apps before you leave wi-fi areas.

MONEY

Larger towns along Ruta 2 such as San Isidro de General and Buenos Aires have ATMs. Puerto Jiménez has two ATMs.

WHERE TO STAY

Town/Village	Pro/Con
Providencia de Dota	Peaceful village tucked away in the highlands. Rural and communal.
San Gerardo de Rivas	Perfect for cloud forest hikes and birdwatching.
Puerto Jiménez	Centrally located for various ecotourism and rural activities. Has an airport and ATMs.

EATING & DRINKING

Providencia and the Los Santos region are renowned for their coffee (pictured top left). Visit CoopeDota, a local coffee cooperative based in Santa María, for a plantation tour and tasting. Visitors to Península de Osa should try the ink-colored *piangua ceviche* (pictured bottom left). This local specialty is made from a mollusk that lives in the Pacific's mangroves.

Best health food
Kapi Kapi Eco
Mercado (p234)

Must-try seafood
Soda Marbella
(p234)

GETTING AROUND

Car and bus

Driving via car or bus is the only way to navigate southern Costa Rica's highlands and cloud forests. Rental cars are available at the Puerto Jiménez airport and allow access to areas not directly reachable by bus.

Boat You can reach Bahía Drake via motorboat through Rio Sierpe. Bahía Drake is walkable and many excursions are by boat.

JAN–APR
Peak summer; it's dry season and thus busiest

MAY–AUG
Mix of rain and sun; possible flooding in June

SEP–OCT
Rainiest season; flooding likely; some businesses close

NOV–DEC
Summer begins; busy season

42 Quetzals & COFFEE

QUETZALS | WATERFALLS | COFFEE

Experience Costa Rica's highlands – one of the only place in Costa Rica to spot quetzals and where the best coffee is grown and harvested. This distinct mountain region is a corridor for tapir, pumas and birds traveling coast to coast, and boasts crisp fresh air and Costa Rica's cleanest river. Providencia de Dota is a departure from expected rainforest experiences.

TANGUY DE SAINT-CYR/SHUTTERSTOCK ©

How To

Getting around A car is necessary due to the winding and mostly unpaved mountain roads. A 4WD is essential during rainy season, but is a good idea year round.

When to go Dry season (January to April) is the best time to go to avoid flooding. The minimal fog and clouds means unobstructed views of the lush valleys and mountains, oceans in the distance and a brilliant night sky.

JANNA ZINZI/LONELY PLANET ©

Quetzals This region is home to **Parque Nacional Los Quetzales** and it is one of the few places in Costa Rica to view these mystical, colorful birds, known as 'Gods of the Wind' by the Maya. Unlike toucans or macaws, which are ubiquitous across the country, quetzals congregate in this area because the aguadillo trees, their main food source, are plentiful. Sunrise hikes in the park or on private farms are the most advantageous ways to catch a glimpse of these vibrant birds. If you're lucky, you'll see the 'machos' or male birds with their turquoise wings and red breasts flying among the trees, feeding themselves or attracting a female mate.

Rivers and waterfalls Four rivers flow through Providencia de Dota creating numerous opportunities to see waterfalls. A 3km hike through the *páramo* grasslands and a mossy cloud forest leads to majestic **La Catarata Divina de Providencia** and the gushing **Río Roncador**. For a more relaxed experience, pack a picnic for **El Salitre**, a small double waterfall that isn't swimmable but is quite mesmerizing. Or take a brisk dip at **Catarata El Pocerón**, a popular swimming hole close to the main road.

Coffee Don't leave without trying and buying some locally grown and harvested coffee from the CoopeDota cooperative sold throughout town. CoopeDota unites local coffee-farming families to ensure everyone is paid fairly for their cultivation.

Top left Resplendent quetzal **Bottom left** Catarata El Pocerón **Above** Puma

ⓘ **Be Part of the Family**

Visiting Providencia not only supports local families and projects, but also is a way for us to share our culture and community. We love making cultural connections with visitors and new people because it's difficult for us to travel and get to know other countries. The families in our community are *pura vida* and truly know the rich natural beauty that surrounds us.

■ **By David Retana,** *Providencia's only local tour guide and extreme biker*
ⓘ *retanadav1d*

Hiking in the
CLOUDS

MOUNTAINS | HIKING | CLOUD FOREST

San Gerardo de Rivas is home to Costa Rica's highest peak, Cerro Chirripó, which stands tall amid the stunning Cordillera de Talamanca mountain range. This quaint town attracts hikers excited to summit Cerro Chirripó and welcomes nature enthusiasts seeking cloud forest and birdwatching adventures. Afterward, relax in thermal pools alongside epic mountain views.

MAX ILLY/EYEEM/GETTY IMAGES ©

🗺️ How To

Getting around Driving is the best way to explore this mountain town and the surrounding sights.

When to go January through April (dry season) is best for ensuring dry hikes and clear skies to take in the grand views.

Viewpoints Part of the route from San José on the Interamericana (Ruta 2) includes Cerro de la Muerte (Death Mountain) known for its dangerous curves, blind spots and monumental views of the Talamanca Mountains.

ALISA.CH/SHUTTERSTOCK ©

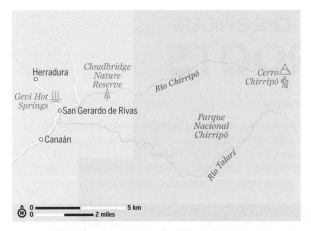

Top left Cerro Chirripó **Bottom left** Cloudbridge Nature Reserve

Cerro Chirripó A bucket-list experience for hiking aficionados, Cerro Chirripó is 3820m above sea level. On a clear day, you can see both the Caribbean and Pacific Oceans. Most people take two days for the hike, spending the night at a base camp 5km from the summit and watching the sun rise from the top the following morning. This hike and entrance to the Parque Nacional Chirripó are only accessible with a guide, and reservations are required. It gets booked out quickly because only 50 people are allowed at one time. Reserve a spot at least six months in advance, especially if planning to visit during the high (dry) season.

Cloudbridge Nature Reserve This reserve adjacent to Parque Nacional Chirripó offers day hikes ranging from moderate to strenuous among picturesque landscapes. Cloudbridge is a 700-acre privately owned nature reserve dedicated to conservation of primary forests and the reforestation of the cloud forest. It's also a research and education center where scientists and volunteers come to study the unique cloud forest ecosystems. Every type of hiker can enjoy the land: there are leisurely 600m trails with scenic waterfalls as well as rugged 8km treks on which you can train for Chirripó.

Gevi Hot Springs For a more relaxing excursion, visit these hot springs where two thermal pools overlook the area's vast mountains and valleys.

🏔 Overnight at Height

Stay for two nights instead of one to have more time to explore Cerro Chirripó. If you summit one day and then descend the next, you miss out on some unique trails around the peak and the base camp, and it can feel rushed. It's a long and strenuous hike to base camp and then to summit, so it's worth giving yourself an extra day to enjoy the views and hike some of the less-populated trails before heading back down the mountain.

■ **By David Elizando,** *owner of Hotel de Montaña el Pelicano and long time guide for Cerro Chirripó* ⓘ *hotelpelicano*

44 Indigenous **ROOTS**

HISTORY | CULTURE | COMMUNITY

▬▬ Costa Rica's past and present meet in the indigenous communities of Térraba, situated amid the Talamanca Mountains. Connect with Brörán and Boruca families through cacao, mask making and weaving workshops that carry on ancestral traditions and exemplify living in concert with nature. Pre-Colombian sites and museums provide a window onto the local culture.

AGEFOTOSTOCK/ALAMY STOCK PHOTO ©

🗺 **How To**

Getting around Renting a car is the only way to fully explore this region since the communities are spread out and public transportation is minimal or nonexistent.

When to go December through April is dry season, guaranteeing sunny days, clearer nights and smoother travel along the serpentine mountain roads. Expect rain during May through November, particularly causing landslides and treacherous roads in September and October.

Workshops Book them via lokaltravel.com.

JUAN CARLOS MUNOZ/ALAMY STOCK PHOTO ©

Far left Boruca masks **Bottom left** Carving Boruca masks **Near left** Museo Boruca

Cacao Learning about cacao from the Brörán people, in Térraba village, is distinct from other workshops geared towards tourists throughout Costa Rica. Cacao is a sacred plant of high value, which cannot be separated from its place as part of the Brörán people's history. You'll participate in the full cacao process, from picking the fruit to roasting and shelling the beans, and grinding the beans using a stone grinder as their ancestors once did. The payoff is a delicious warm chocolate beverage and conversation with the family.

Museum In the Boruca community, a small museum gives insight into pre-colonial life through replicas of their living quarters and cooking tools. One of the Pre-Columbian stone spheres is on display along with powerful art depicting their gods, goddesses and warriors. Visitors can also attend mask-making and weaving workshops led by local Boruca artisans. Watch these skilled craftspeople make intricate masks out of cedar depicting nature motifs and fierce warrior faces. This honors their ancestors who fought the Spanish conquistadors, and the masks are used for festivals in late December and early January re-enacting the bravery of their forefathers.

Weaving Workshops demonstrate the impressive complexity of weaving the various threads on an imposing loom, as well as seeing how the Boruca use various plants and natural materials, such as turmeric and *mata azul*, to dye their thread. Gorgeous colorful bags, wallets and table runners are for sale directly from women artisans or at the museum.

(i) A Continuing Legacy

A lot of the conversation about indigenous people, our tribes and families talks about us as if we were completely annihilated or extinct. We are talked about in the past tense and our presence is erased. But we are here, building our communities and keeping our traditions alive. My family and I love to host travelers from all over the world to share our culture on the land of my great-grandparents. We hope more visitors to Costa Rica will come learn about our rich history and how we are continuing the legacy of our ancestors.

■ **By Jeffrey Villanueva,** *Brörán community leader and owner of El Descanso Terraba facebook.com/ eldescansoterraba*

45

Under the
SEA

DIVING | SNORKELING | MARINE LIFE

▬▬▬ Península de Osa is a haven for scuba divers because of its crystal waters and impressive underwater views. Isla del Caño, near Bahía Drake, is a marine biological reserve teeming with coral, turtles and tropical fish, while Golfo Dulce, near Puerto Jiménez, is one of four tropical fjords on the planet. Dolphin and whale sightings are common and absolutely awe-inspiring.

WATERFRAME/ALAMY STOCK PHOTO ©

🏝 How To

Getting here/around
Driving between Bahía Drake (Drake Bay) and Puerto Jiménez takes about 1½ hours on bumpy, dirt roads. A 4WD is ideal. Both places have airports and are a 20-minute flight apart.

Take the motorboat ferry to Bahía Drake from Sierpe for a seafaring adventure.

When to go Peak diving season is January through June when underwater visibility is best. During rainy season, the water will likely be murky, limiting visibility.

DAVE HAMILTON/GETTY IMAGES ©

Isla del Caño Scuba divers flock to Bahía Drake to dive at Isla del Caño, a world-renowned marine reserve with excellent visibility during diving season. It's common to swim among various marine critters, such as whale sharks, bull sharks, octopuses, sea turtles, rays and dozens of species of fish. Beginner and expert divers will enjoy exploring the wondrous caves and sprawling coral reefs.

The 300-hectare island holds centuries of Costa Rica's indigenous history. It was a burial ground for the Chiriquis people and contains pre-Colombian stone spheres like the ones found on the mainland (south of Palmar Norte) at **El Sitio Museo Finca 6**, the museum dedicated to these structures. Tourists have not been permitted to visit the island since the onset of COVID-19, but the surrounding waters are the main attraction.

Golfo Dulce On the other side of Península de Osa, you'll find Golfo Dulce, one of only four tropical fjords in the world. It's a snorkeling utopia teeming with schools of dolphins and groups of sea turtles. Golfo Dulce is a sanctuary for various shark species and for humpback whales, who use it as a breeding ground to raise their offspring. Parque Nacional Corcovado and Parque National Piedras Blancas border this body of water offering spectacular verdant views of the lush Península de Osa from your boat. Some of the surrounding beaches are designated Blue Flag (Bandera Azul), meaning they are nationally recognized for their cleanliness.

Top left Isla del Caño **Bottom left** Pantropical spotted dolphins, Golfo Dulce

 Packing Pro Tips

Be prepared for this tropical rainforest climate by protecting yourself from the sun and the bugs. Make sure you have reef-safe sunscreen, a long-sleeved shirt, sunglasses and a hat that covers your face and neck. Have water shoes for Golfo Dulce adventures, and don't forget water to drink!

 ■ **By Yesenia Quintero,** *tour guide and owner of Zompopas Tours, Playa Blanca, Península de Osa* ⊙ *zompopas_trails_costa_rica*

46
Waterfalls & **WHALES**

WHALE-WATCHING | WATERFALLS | NIGHT TOURS

▬▬▬ Bahía Drake (pictured below) offers a plethora of opportunities to experience the region's biodiversity. Explore this remote bay and the surrounding areas via these nature adventures, which showcase the splendor of the Península de Osa.

STEFAN NEUMANN/ SHUTTERSTOCK ©

🗺 Trip Notes

Getting here/around Skip driving a rental car here and take the ferry via Sierpe. Bahía Drake (Drake Bay) township is walkable and many excursions provide transportation.

When to go Although dry season (December through April) offers the best weather, it's the most crowded time. Consider visiting in May, July and November. You may get some rain, but it won't last all day, and there will be fewer tourists.

Footwear Bring sturdy hiking boots and waterproof sandals!

🐚 Night Moves

Living on the Península de Osa means that just beyond the next mud puddle or tropical tree, there's a chance to slip into whole new worlds of wonder – bundles that creep, crawl and fly by night. So pack a headlamp. Exploring the forest at night will reveal creatures never seen by day.

■ **By Tracie Stice,** 'The Bug Lady,' biologist and night tour guide in Bahía Drake
@drake.sachatamia

01 Take a boat tour along **Río Sierpe**, the gateway to Bahía Drake. Among the plentiful mangroves, you'll see great blue herons (pictured left), monos titi (squirrel monkeys), toucans, crocodiles and other creatures.

Bahía de Coronado

Sierpe

Río Sierpe

03 There's an extraordinary world of reptiles, insects and mammals lurking in the dark. Tracie the Bug Lady's **night tour** will give you a deep appreciation for the region's nocturnal wildlife.

Bahía Drake

Reserva Forestal Golfo Dulce

02 Migrating whales breed and have their babies in Bahía Drake. Numerous **whale-watching** excursions are available, and the best time to see humpbacks is mid-July through mid-October.

○ Drake

● Agujitas

Parque Nacional Corcovado

04 Drive inland to Los Planes and Naguala Eco-Lodge where you can spend the day hiking along the Río Aguitas and exploring **Naguala Falls**.

Península de Osa

0 10 km
0 5 miles

47 Live Like a
LOCAL

NATURE | CULTURE | ECOTOURISM

Rural ecotourism excursions give you an eye into local Tico life, culture and history. Get to know Costa Rica and the people outside of the popular tourist attractions and typical tropical activities. Connecting with locals who know and love their land offers an enriching opportunity to build understanding across borders while having a lot of fun.

TIM FLEMING/ALAMY STOCK PHOTO ©

🗺 How To

Getting here/around
Renting a car is the best way to approach these rural regions. As always, get a car with 4WD to cope with unpaved roads. Also download any maps in advance since cell service is limited.

When to go For the best weather, visit from January through April to avoid torrential rains.

Tip Always try the locally grown produce!

JEAN BAPTISTE TOUSSAINT/SHUTTERSTOCK ©

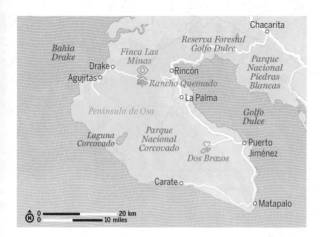

Rancho Quemado A small and quaint village, Rancho Quemado is located about 45 minutes from the Bahía Drake (Drake Bay) coast. The people here have opened up their homes to create sustainable ecotourism experiences that show tourists what daily life is like outside of the beaches and national parks. Travelers can visit farms and take meandering boat tours for birdwatching. Or you can fish in a local *laguna*, milk cows, or take a cooking class.

Finca Las Minas A highlight is coming here where you can try mining for gold in a local creek. The owner, Don Juan Cubrillo, shares the history of gold mining and its significance to the region as well as information about his indigenous heritage. He then guides you to the nearby river where you witness and experience panning for gold in the iron-rich ochre soil. Afterwards, his wife Rosa blesses you with a delicious and hearty home-cooked meal from their outdoor kitchen using local ingredients.

Dos Brazos About a 45-minute drive from Puerto Jiménez, Dos Brazos also offers travelers rural adventures. The area contains farms, hidden waterfalls, ecolodges and another entrance to the El Tigre sector of Parque Nacional Corcovado. Local experts offer tours for birdwatching and to learn about medicinal plants, or you can hike through the rainforest to visit with locals living there. You'll learn about their lives and the region over home-cooked meals and cultural exchange.

Top left Península de Osa **Bottom left** Scarlet macaw

🌱 Dos Brazos

Dos Brazos is a small and tranquil rural community. It does not get crowded so you can really enjoy nature and get to know the people. You can bathe and swim in the river, and drink the water. It comes from the mountain, more delicious than bottled water! Tourism is a growing industry for us and we have so much knowledge to share about the rich history of this land and especially the plants.

■ **By Esther Coronado,** *president of Acodobrarti, Corcovado el Tigre, a local conservation organization* @corcovadoeltigre

48

Welcome to the
JUNGLE

HIKING | WILDLIFE | NATURE

▬▬▬ Parque Nacional Corcovado contains 2.5% of the world's biodiversity. On entering this remote park, the unique flora and fauna are on full display. Full-day hikes traverse rainforests and rivers amid various species of remarkable birds, mammals and reptiles.

🗺️ How To

Getting here/around
To reach La Leona entrance, drive two hours along unpaved rocky roads from Puerto Jiménez to Carate. A 4WD is necessary. Some travelers hire drivers; others do it themselves. La Sirena entrance is reached via motorboat from Puerto Jiménez and a wet landing on the beach (exiting the boat in the water near the shore).

When to go Visiting between December and April ensures dry trails and ample animal sightings. Avoid September and October when heavy rains cause flooding and thus road and park closures.

Protecting the Environment

Preserving the pristine natural ecosystems of **Parque Nacional Corcovado** is a top priority. Therefore a guide is required to enter the park, so it's best to book a tour instead of trying to do it yourself. Also, when entering the park at any station, rangers check bags to make sure no one brings in any food, and thus garbage. This ensures the park stays clean and the animals don't start expecting to be fed, becoming aggressive toward humans.

Rise & Shine

The best time to visit is early morning when the animals are most active and before the hottest time of the day. A 45-minute boat ride launches your Corcovado adventure when visiting the La Sirena sector. Keep your eyes open for whales and dolphins along the way.

🧍 Park Tips

Bring plenty of water with you into the park, especially during the hot and humid dry season. Also make sure to have solid footwear meaning sturdy hiking boots with traction that can handle various terrain or rubber boots, which are useful for crossing rivers and avoiding snakes on the path.

Top left Parque Nacional Corcovado
Top right Trogon **Bottom left** La Sirena ranger station (p227)

After a bumpy drive to Carate, a splendid yet steamy 3.5km beach walk to La Leona ranger station takes you to the entrance of the park. Shadier forest paths are a reprieve from the direct sun to explore the trails where the animals camouflage into the surroundings.

Choose Your Route

Most visitors take day trips to either La Sirena sector or La Leona sector, but those wanting a more immersive experience stay overnight in the park. Two- and three-day **hiking routes** include the 20km trail from Carate/La Leona to La Sirena ranger station where you spend the night, followed by hiking one of seven

⚠⚠ Immerse Yourself in Nature

If you want to visit Parque Nacional Corcovado, the best experience is an overnight tour, which can be two days/one night or three days/two nights. Other excellent options that are less-saturated with tourists are day tours of La Leona sector, or El Tigre sector, which is managed by the local community. I would put the option of Sirena from Drake Bay or Puerto Jiménez last, especially in high season, because it is too crowded and overwhelming. The magic of Corcovado is lost with so many people on the same trail.

■ Recommended by Ifigenia Garita Canet, *tropical biologist and Founder of Osa Wild* osawild

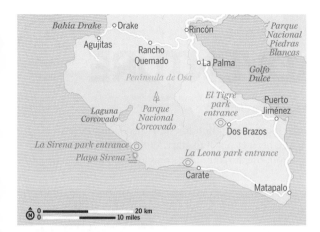

Left Spider monkey, Parque Nacional Corcovado **Below** Baird's tapir

trails in La Sirena sector the next day. La Sirena ranger station has dormitory-style lodging with clean shared bathrooms, a dining hall, and a small shop with souvenirs, coffee and first-aid items.

Access to the sandy beach walk from La Leona to La Sirena depends on the tide, and includes river crossings and inclines once you're in the park. The intensity ranges from moderate to strenuous depending on the conditions, so it's not recommended for beginner hikers.

Rare Sights

Parque Nacional Corcovado is world renowned for its biodiversity and you will be up close and personal with wildlife. One of the most famed animal residents is the tapir, a relatively rare herbivore mammal. They are most active in the morning or evening when they are gathering food, but a good tour guide will usually help you spot one sleeping in the bushes after its meal. Noisy howler monkeys and their spider monkey cousins will swing above you; and wild turkeys, peccaries and coatis will cross your path. You may see crocodiles gliding through the Rio Claro or hear the squawking scarlet macaws as they fly overhead.

49 Osa **ADVENTURE**

CHOCOLATE | SLOTHS | BIOLUMINESCENCE

Península de Osa is the ideal destination for slow travel, and Puerto Jiménez (pictured below) is the perfect place to start. While Parque Nacional Corcovado is the main attraction, the surrounding areas are rich with exciting ecotourism adventures.

JEMZUFE/ SHUTTERSTOCK ©

(i) Puerto Jiménez

Jiménez, as the locals affectionately call it, is the main hub of the Península de Osa. It serves as a great launching pad for exploration. Transportation around the Osa can be difficult and expensive. If you are comfortable driving on dirt roads, renting a 4WD vehicle will open up the entire peninsula for you.

🗺 Trip Notes

Getting around Rent a car from the Puerto Jiménez airport to best explore various parts of the Península de Osa.

When to go December through April offers the best weather, but also the most crowds. Visit instead during the low season to avoid crowds. But avoid September and October when heavy rain could ruin your plans.

Travel time Give yourself ample time to travel and take in each destination.

■ By Eytan Elterman, *co-founder of Lokal Travel* ⊚ *lokaltravels*

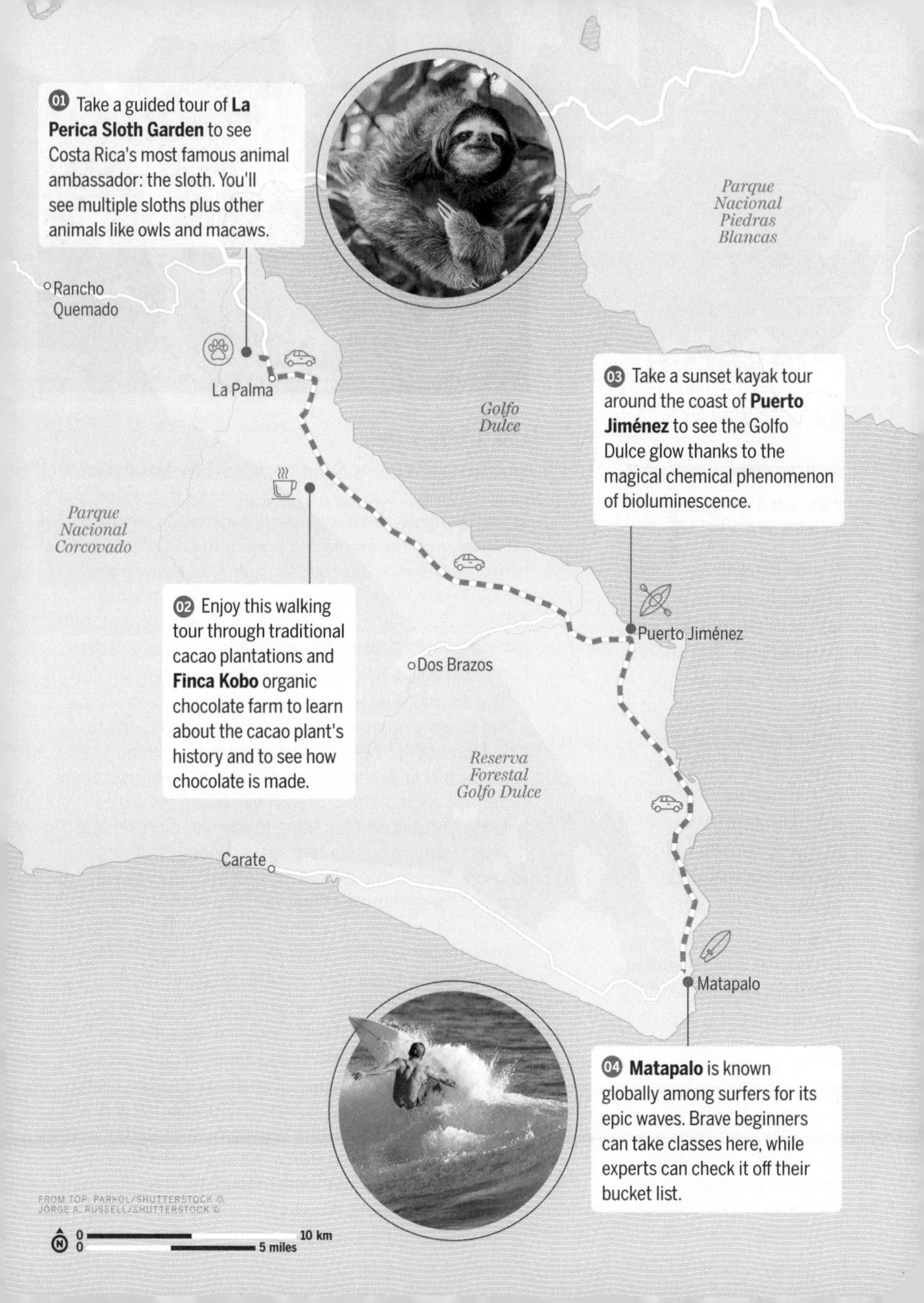

01 Take a guided tour of **La Perica Sloth Garden** to see Costa Rica's most famous animal ambassador: the sloth. You'll see multiple sloths plus other animals like owls and macaws.

Rancho Quemado

Parque Nacional Piedras Blancas

La Palma

Golfo Dulce

03 Take a sunset kayak tour around the coast of **Puerto Jiménez** to see the Golfo Dulce glow thanks to the magical chemical phenomenon of bioluminescence.

Parque Nacional Corcovado

02 Enjoy this walking tour through traditional cacao plantations and **Finca Kobo** organic chocolate farm to learn about the cacao plant's history and to see how chocolate is made.

Dos Brazos

Puerto Jiménez

Reserva Forestal Golfo Dulce

Carate

Matapalo

04 **Matapalo** is known globally among surfers for its epic waves. Brave beginners can take classes here, while experts can check it off their bucket list.

N

0 | 10 km
0 | 5 miles

Preserve & Protect

CARING FOR THE LANDS WE VISIT

Costa Rica is a global leader in conservation and ecotourism due to its extraordinary biodiversity. Even as much of the land is protected, the allure of experiencing these natural resources attracts tourists from all over the world. How can travelers engage with Costa Rica's distinct climate while honoring and respecting the land?

Costs & Benefits

Much of Costa Rica's allure lies in its unmatched natural environment. It's a major selling point for its tourism marketing, as ecotourism is a burgeoning national industry. However, with the increasing popularity of Costa Rica's nature adventures, mass tourism puts these environments at risk. This is felt acutely in Península de Osa, which *National Geographic* named 'the most biologically intense place on Earth,' and where multinational hotel corporations with political backing are looking to expand.

The southern region and Península de Osa encompass a vast range of climates, from mountain highlands to cloud forests to tropical rainforests and beaches. The landscape is lush, the water fresh and the air crisp. Local experts in each of these areas have noted the delicate balance between encouraging tourism and preserving the habitat. Tourism boosts the local economy and is a means to share culture and educate visitors about the land. Yet many of these remote places don't have the infrastructure to sustain the increasing visitor numbers. This can drain natural resources and negatively impact the local families who have built these communities for generations.

San Gerardo de Rivas, for example, has gained popularity for international expats looking for retirement or investment properties. The increase in construction affects the cloud forest microclimate while also raising prices for long-time Tico residents. Another issue is that Parque Nacional Corcovado is becoming a top destination, but the infrastructure in Bahía Drake isn't designed to accommodate large numbers of tourists. Thus electrical

Top left Scarlet macaw **Top center** Tree-climbing crab **Top right** Iguana

blackouts are common. Also, more visitors in the park means more disturbance to the animals and foot traffic on the trails. Although permits are required to visit, Costa Rica hasn't been tracking the number of visitors to monitor the impact. Because Parque Nacional Corcovado houses 2.5% of the world's biodiversity, it's critical that efforts to mitigate the effects of increased tourism are made.

> The landscape is lush, the water fresh and the air crisp. Yet many of these remote places don't have the infrastructure to sustain the increasing visitor numbers.

Climate change is also an undeniable factor and locals talk about it as a grave threat to the country's unique ecosystems. But when compounded with mass tourism, the environmental impact is even greater. Mass tourism necessitates more highways, hotels and disturbing of the land. Higher temperatures and overdeveloped land definitely shifts already fragile conditions.

Conscious Travelers

As conscious travelers, we can be intentional in how we show up. There are simple things we can do such as bringing reusable water bottles to eliminate single-use plastic bottles and picking up your trash (and others') when on the beach. We can also patronize hotels and restaurants owned by Ticos and/ or use sustainable practices. Lastly, book tours with operators who support local guides and ecotourism excursions that honor the pure splendor of Costa Rica.

ⓘ Sustainable Tourism

In response to the ballooning tourist economy, Costa Rica's tourism board created a Certification for Sustainable Tourism (CST) to evaluate hotels and lodging operators' use of sustainable practices. It's not a perfect measuring stick since it's a voluntary program, but it encourages tourism businesses to consider their impact on their surrounding natural environment and the local community, and how they engage their visitors in conservation efforts. The country's tourism board incentivizes businesses to step up their sustainability practices by offering promotional opportunities and a branded logo that lets consumers know they are making an ecofriendly choice.

SIGHTS
of the South

01 Dolphins
These marine mammals are ubiquitous, swimming in schools throughout Golfo Dulce and Bahía Drake.

02 Macaws
Scarlet macaws are endangered animals, but are ubiquitous on Península de Osa. They mate for life and always fly in pairs.

03 Coffee beans
The Santa María region near Providencia de Dota is where Costa Rica's best coffee is grown.

04 Boruca mask
Indigenous Boruca artists hand-carve and paint these masks to represent their ultural pride and their fight against colonialism.

05 Trap door spider
You only see these nocturnal creatures if you know where to look. They camouflage themselves on mossy surfaces.

06 Mono titi (squirrel monkey)
The smallest of all of Costa Rica's monkeys travel in large groups and are only found in this region.

07 Quetzal
This colorful mythical bird revered by the Maya people can be found in the highlands of Providencia de Dota.

08 Cacao fruit
This plant is sacred to indigenous communities, and visitors can taste it in all forms: beverage, beans and bars.

09 Whales
These massive mammals are a common sight as they migrate up and down the Pacific coast all year long.

10 Diquís spheres
These mysterious stone spheres date back to the Pre-Columbian indigenous societies that lived throughout the region.

Listings

BEST OF THE REST

🍸 Drink Up

DinerCraft Bar and Restaurant $$$

Stop by the bar in Bahía Drake's Hotel Margarita for fresh fruit margaritas and craft cocktails. Stay for an exquisite seafood dinner.

Playa Blanca Beach Bar $

Sip on a cold Pilsen with local Ticos and other tourists as you take in the gorgeous Golfo Dulce scenery.

Batsu Gastropub $$

Taste some Costa Rica craft beers and cocktails made with fresh ingredients at this family-friendly pub and restaurant near Parque Nacional Chirripó.

For the Foodies

Kapi Kapi Eco Mercado $$

Start your day in San Gerardo de Rivas with creative concoctions of fresh fruit, herbs and other locally sourced ingredients. Extensive dinner menu for health-conscious travelers.

Marea Alta $

Visitors and locals in Bahía Drake enjoy delicious food and a great soundtrack. Try the squash ceviche or hefty *casados* (set meals).

Maracaibo Bar & Restaurante $

A fun local hangout in Buenos Aires, near Térraba, with delicious typical Tico cuisine, a full bar and an open-air patio.

Soda Marbella $$

You know it's good because the locals are here. This is the go-to spot in Puerto Jiménez for seafood, especially ceviche.

Kala Luna Bistro $$$

Enjoy a flavorful fusion of Mediterranean and Latin American cuisine at this gourmet restaurant along the coast of Bahía Drake.

Iguana Lodge $$$

Dine beachside overlooking Playa Platanares in Puerto Jiménez. Taste the carrot-pineapple-mango slaw among various other salad and fresh fish options.

Soda Leila $

A great pit-stop after a day of snorkeling and swimming in Playa Blanca. Some of the best *casados* in the area.

Truchero Los Cocolisos $$

Catch your own fish at this trout farm and restaurant in San Gerardo de Rivas. Fun for families and groups who want to try trout prepared in different ways.

Casa el Tortugo Drake's Kitchen $$

Can't go wrong with seafood and ceviche at this riverside family-run restaurant in Bahía Drake. It also has lodging available.

Buena Esperanza (Martina's Bar) $$

If you get hungry on your way to or from Parque Nacional Corcovado, stop at this delightful open-air restaurant near Matapalo. Don't leave without trying the locally made ice cream.

Mon's Shack and Grill House $

Costa Rican *casados* and other specialties abound at this restaurant off of the main road in San Gerardo de Rivas. There's also a working sugar mill pulled by oxen.

Soda Jiménez Colectivo $

Tico home cooking for breakfast, lunch and dinner in Puerto Jiménez. Affordable and filling *casados*, nachos and *empanadas* (turnovers stuffed with meat and cheese) are crowd pleasers.

Mar Luna Lounge $$$

A hidden gem in Playa Tamales with house-made artisanal pizzas, and refreshing cocktails to enjoy poolside.

 Gifts Galore

Puerto Jiménez Souvenir Shop

It's a one-stop shop for goods made by local artisans and farmers. Peruse jewelry, chocolate, bathing suits and more.

Museo Boruca

Support the indigenous Boruca artisans by purchasing woven wallets, bags and home-goods, as well as Boruca masks.

Adventure Time

Senderos Providencia

For the hard-core bikers, join Senderos Providencia on harrowing dirt trails through the Talamanca Mountains of Providencia de Dota.

Psycho Tours

Not your typical tours. Play in nature near Matapalo with guided activities like tree climbing and waterfall rappelling.

Osa Wild

The hub for ecotourism experiences throughout Península de Osa. Based in Puerto Jiménez, Osa Wild can connect you to a variety of outdoor adventures with naturalist expert guides.

Lokal Travels

Comprehensive trip planning focused on ecotourism and rural tourism itineraries

Museo Boruca

that support local businesses, covering Providencia de Dota, San Gerardo de Rivas, Térraba and Península de Osa.

☼ Sand, Swimming & Sunbathing

Playa San Josecito

This quiet, golden-sand beach outside Bahía Drake is perfect for sunbathing and relaxing. Beware of the strong currents when swimming.

Playa Colorada

One of the main beaches in Bahía Drake. There are many restaurants and shops along the shore, but try a ceviche *caldosa* from the family-owned food truck.

Playa Blanca

This beach along the Golfo Dulce is known as one of the cleanest beaches in Costa Rica. A jump-off point for snorkeling tours outside Puerto Jiménez.

Playa Puntarenitas

Enjoy a lazy beach day at this local beach in the center of Puerto Jiménez, with sweeping views of Golfo Dulce.

 Scan to find more things to do in Southern Costa Rica & Península de Osa online

Practicalities

ARRIVING

238

GETTING AROUND

240

SAFE TRAVEL

242

MONEY

243

RESPONSIBLE TRAVEL

244

ACCOMMODATIONS

246

ESSENTIALS

248

LANGUAGE

250

Right Painted wooden wheel from a traditional Costa Rican ox cart

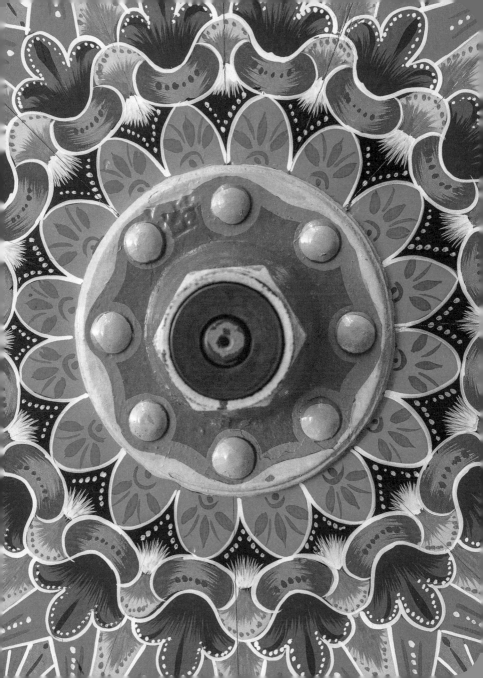

EASY STEPS FROM THE AIRPORT TO THE CITY CENTER

Most travelers visiting the country come through either of the two international airports: Juan Santamaría International Airport (SJO), or Liberia International Airport (LIR) – formerly known as the Daniel Oduber Quirós International Airport – in Liberia, in Costa Rica's northwest. At SJO there are two terminals: the main terminal for international travel and the domestic terminal for short in-country flights.

AT THE AIRPORT

GIANFRANCO VIVI/SHUTTERSTOCK ©

SIM CARDS
At SJO, there's a Claro SIM card stand in baggage claim where you can purchase a prepaid Costa Rican SIM card. It's open daily from 5am to 9pm and later on weekends. There's nowhere to buy a SIM card at LIR, so go to a cellphone store or supermarket.

CURRENCY EXCHANGE
There are 24-hour Global Exchange counters in the lobby and boarding area and at baggage-claim carousels 3 and 5 at SJO. At LIR there are Global Exchange counters in the lobby, customs, baggage claim and by international departures.

DUTY FREE Travelers are allowed to purchase 400 cigarettes or 50 cigars or 500g tobacco. Travelers over 18 can bring 5L of alcoholic beverages (usually two bottles).

ATMS At SJO there are two ATMs: one in the baggage-claim area, the other by departures. At LIR, there's an ATM in the arrivals hall. All take Visa/Mastercard.

CHARGING STATIONS Electrical outlets are plentiful at SJO. At LIR the best place to charge your phone is in a lounge.

WI-FI
At SJO, free wi-fi is available for three hours by connecting to the Free SJO Wi-fi by Samsung network. There is also a premium paid wi-fi service available. At LIR, there's free wi-fi. It's not the fastest, but it works if you need to arrange an Uber or check reservations.

GETTING TO SAN JOSÉ CITY CENTER

UBER Readily available at SJO airport and are generally more cost-effective than taxis. It costs roughly US$12 to US$18 without surging prices to get to the city center and takes anywhere from 30 to 50 minutes depending on traffic.

BUS For a cheaper option, the Tuasa bus and the Station Wagon bus offer services between the airport and downtown San José. They cost around US$1 and take about 30 minutes. Both buses stop across the street from the main arrivals terminal.

TRAIN Taking a train is the least desirable option because you'll need to take a taxi or rideshare 2.5km to the Alajuela railway station to ride to downtown San José. It takes 50 minutes. and a one-way ticket costs approximately US$1.75.

HOW MUCH FOR A

Uber
US$15
30 minutes

bus
US$1
30 minutes

train
US$1.75
50 minutes

SHUTTLES

Various travel companies offer direct shuttle buses (US$23 to US$35) to the city center and its hotels. It's a 35-minute ride.

DOMESTIC TERMINALS

If you fly into the domestic terminal, the ride-share pick-up location is a five-minute walk from the terminal's exit.

TAXIS These are available at the airport, but will probably cost more than Uber because they run on a meter.

OTHER POINTS OF ENTRY

Liberia's city center is a 10-minute drive from the airport; however, most visitors flying into Liberia International Airport (LIR) head the other direction to the beaches and towns on the Pacific coast. The airport is an hour's drive from Tamarindo and two hours from Nosara. Uber is available, but most visitors rent cars and drive to their destinations. Numerous car-rental agencies offer free shuttles from the airport to their nearby car centers.

Various shared and private shuttle services are available to hotels in Tamarindo, Papagayo, Playas del Coco, Sámara and other popular beach locations. They should be booked online in advance and will be waiting for you at the airport. A public bus to Liberia from the airport will cost about US$1.

Travelers also enter Costa Rica via cruises to ports in Puntarenas on the Pacific coast and Limón City on the Caribbean coast. Road trippers can enter via bus or car from the northern border with Nicaragua or the southern border with Panama. You'll need to show a plane, bus or cruise ticket showing your exit out of Costa Rica within the 90-day visit limit.

TRANSPORT TIPS TO HELP YOU GET AROUND

Renting a car allows you to explore different parts of the country at your own pace. Most visitors rent a car from San José and drive to their destination. For long-distance journeys, such as traveling to Limón City or Puerto Jiménez, it's best to fly in and then rent a car. Having a car is convenient in places without Uber or metered taxis.

BUYER BEWARE Some rental-car companies advertize very low prices. However, once you arrive there are often high fees for required insurance and large deposits on your credit card to book the car. There's no getting around paying for third-party liability insurance, so shop around.

TUK-TUK On the southern Caribbean coast, tuk-tuks are a great way to travel around Puerto Viejo and to the smaller beach towns to the south. The cost of a ride depends on the distance, but short rides tend to be about 1000 colones (US$1.50).

BUSES

Buses are a low-cost way to travel throughout the country. Private companies operate the buses depending on the region and thus bus condition varies. Know the name of the company you're traveling with because each company has its own bus stop.

FERRY

Many ferries are more like motorboats than barges. Certain places like the village of Tortuguero, and thus its national park, are only accessible via ferry. There are also car ferries between Puerto Jiménez and Golfito, and between Puntarenas and Península de Nicoya. This option may cut driving time, but schedules can be limited.

CAR RENTAL PER DAY

Sedan
US$15 to US$65

SUV
US$25 to US$75

Pick-up truck
US$65+

RENTAL-CAR TIP Make sure to rent a car that has 4WD, especially if you're traveling during rainy season (June through November) or planning to drive in more rural or remote areas. These vehicles tend to be listed as medium SUVs. It's a good rule of thumb to have a 4WD for most road trips in Costa Rica considering some roads may be unpaved or there may be stream and river crossings.

DRIVING ESSENTIALS

Costa Rica drives on the right side of the road.

Most highways have one lane.

The normal speed limit on the highway is 90km/h (56mph).

18 The legal driving age is 18, but to rent a car it's usually 21 to 23.

Road signs are in Spanish and have similar symbols to the USA and Canada.

INSURANCE When renting a car you're legally required to pay for third-party liability insurance, so add an extra US$12 to US$20 a day to any online quotes. If your credit card provides collision insurance, you needn't take out that coverage with the rental agency; however, some car-rental operators require a letter from your credit-card company to confirm. Check with your credit-card company before you leave. When booking online, some companies are explicit about additional fees, while others spring them on you at the rental counter.

ROAD CONDITIONS When driving in the mountains be on the alert for *derrumbes* (landslides), particularly during or after rain. They are particularly common during rainy season (July through November). Also, rainy season can make unpaved roads more treacherous, and flood river crossings. Be wise about whether or not it's safe to cross a flowing river, and do not risk it. Sometimes there are construction crews repairing the road, so you'll have to stop.

PLANES Domestic flights are a quick way to get to more remote places. These propeller planes usually carry 20 to 25 people, which may be unnerving for those used to much larger planes. Enjoy the breathtaking views and avoiding long drives, bumpy roads and traffic.

ROAD DISTANCE CHART (KMS)

	Cahuita	Jacó	La Fortuna	Limón City	Manuel Antonio	Manzanillo	Puerto Viejo	San José	Tamarindo
Jacó	300								
La Fortuna	255	150							
Limón City	45	255	215						
Manuel Antonio	320	70	220	265					
Manzanillo	30	330	285	75	340				
Puerto Viejo	20	320	270	60	320	15			
San José	200	100	130	160	140	235	220		
Tamarindo	460	235	210	415	300	490	485	260	
Uvita	350	125	275	310	65	385	370	220	360

KNOW YOUR CARBON FOOTPRINT

A domestic round-trip flight from SJO to Limón City would emit 197kg of carbon dioxide per passenger. A SUV or van would emit 71kg for the same distance.

A domestic round-trip flight from SJO to Puerto Jiménez would emit 213kg of carbon dioxide per passenger. A SUV or van would emit 152kg for the same distance.

SAFE TRAVEL

Costa Rica is a generally safe country for travelers. As with most destinations, use common sense to protect yourself from theft by securing your wallets and purses, and not leaving your stuff unattended on the beach.

DENGUE FEVER

This painful viral infection, transmitted by mosquitos, will ruin your vacation. The best way to prevent dengue is using bug repellent, especially at sunset when mosquitos are most active.

FAKE TAXIS There's a common scam targeting solo travelers waiting at bus stops. If you're at a bus stop, do not get into a 'taxi' that tells you the bus has already left or there's a strike, and offers to take you to the next stop. The driver will take you to an ATM to extort money.

SEX TOURISM Sex work is legal in Costa Rica, so it's a popular destination for sex tourism. San José and Jacó are particularly known for their abundance of sex workers. Women travelers, especially solo, should do research before booking hotels because some are known to cater specifically for sex tourism.

DRUGS Medical marijuana is legal, but recreational marijuana is illegal, even though you'll smell it everywhere. Drug possession for immediate personal use is decriminalized, but police may stop and search you, and it's up to their discretion what constitutes 'personal use.' Cocaine and hallucinogens are plentiful. Use at your own risk.

PLANT MEDICINE

Many travelers are interested in trying plant medicine like ayahuasca. These plants can have powerful effects on those who consume them, so do your research on who is administering the ceremony and their plan for health emergencies.

DRIVING ETIQUETTE Don't be alarmed if a driver tailgates you before overtaking. It can be stressful but it's a customary practice when locals pass slower-moving drivers – and is seldom done with aggressive intent.

WOLLERTZ/SHUTTERSTOCK ©

NOBITO/SHUTTERSTOCK ©

VOLCANOES Costa Rica has five active volcanos. Travelers aren't usually in danger from eruptions, but parks may be closed. Research before heading out.

QUICK TIPS TO HELP YOU MANAGE YOUR MONEY

ATMS Banco Nacional and Banco de Costa Rica (BCR) are the most ubiquitous banks and ATMs. In San José, you'll find international banks like HSBC and Scotiabank. Most ATMs offer the option of Spanish or English, and the option of colones or dollars. Most cities and towns have ATMs; however, rural areas, even if tourist-friendly, may not. Always have cash on you.

CURRENCY

Costa Rica's national currency is colones. US dollars are widely accepted in most tourist destinations, but you'll get more for your money by paying in colones.

CREDIT CARDS

Visa and Mastercard are accepted by most businesses around the country. Major hotel or rental-car chains may accept American Express. Always carry some cash.

CURRENCY

colones (₡)

HOW MUCH FOR A

Cup of coffee
US$1

Guaro sour
US$3

Casado
US$5-8

TIPPING Tipping is not customary in Costa Rica; however, on average tourists tip 10% for services like tour guides or drivers. In tourist areas, you will see tip jars. Tip in colones as it's the local currency.

VAT

Value-added tax (13%) is added in stores, hotels and restaurants. Usually it's already factored into tour and excursion prices. Restaurants are also required to charge a 10% service tax, which may not be included in menu prices.

THE COLOR OF MONEY

Costa Rican currency is pretty! Each bill is a different color with a different local animal represented. One has monkeys, another has sloths, and another morphos (blue butterflies synonymous with Costa Rica).

EATING ON A BUDGET Costa Rica is the most expensive country in Central America, and visitors are often shocked by the prices, especially at restaurants. To stretch your budget, book a hotel that includes breakfast. A typical local breakfast consists of Costa Rica's national dish, *gallo pinto* (a hearty mix of white rice and black beans), eggs, *natilla* (sour cream) and fried sweet plantains, plus coffee and juice. You'll save money and be full for hours.

NATURE ON A BUDGET If you're interested in visiting multiple national parks, consider a membership to the Amigos de los Parques Nacionales. This organization offers a couple of packages that provide discounts on admission fees and also support its conservation non-profit. Twelve national parks are included in the pass.

RESPONSIBLE TRAVEL

Tips to leave a lighter footprint, support local and have a positive impact on local communities.

JARNOGZ/GETTY IMAGES ©

ON THE ROAD

Cycle or walk when you can. Many popular tourist locations are walkable or have bikes available for rent to explore the surrounding areas.

Travel with tour groups for excursions instead of taking a rental car. Carpooling is better for the environment!

Bring a reusable cloth shopping bag to reduce your single-plastic use. Recycling is limited in many parts of the country.

Use reef-safe sunscreen. Protect Costa Rica's beautiful and rare coral reefs, which are essential to global ocean health, when swimming, snorkeling or doing any water activities.

Leave it better than you found it. Volunteer with a local conservation group, or do an informal beach clean up by picking up garbage on the sand whenever possible.

Turn off the lights, fans and A/C when you're out and about to reduce electricity usage.

GIVE BACK

Cloudbridge Nature Reserve is dedicated to protecting the cloud forest in the Cordillera de Talamanca. While many biologists conduct research there, volunteers need no formal education or experience. Volunteers help in various ways: planting trees, greeting visitors and maintaining trails. cloudbridge.org/ volunteering/volunteer-opportunities

The Sea Turtle Conservancy offers a Turtle Eco-Volunteer Program for eight days during nesting season from June through November. Volunteers help count eggs, record data and measure turtles. stcturtle.org/green-turtle-eco-volunteer-program

Proyecto Asis is dedicated to the conservation of local wild animals. Individuals and families can volunteer by preparing food for the animals, cleaning the enclosures, repairing and building enclosures, and making environmental enrichment toys for the rescue animals. institutoasis.com/volunteer_service_program

DON'T FEED THE MONKEYS!

The cara blanca monkeys (white-faced monkeys) in the national parks are used to being fed by tourists, who think they are cute animals. But they will get aggressive and travel in groups. Make sure your bags are secured and closed at parks and beaches.

LEAVE A SMALL FOOTPRINT

Stay at ecofriendly lodgings. Many hotels have enacted sustainable practices, including using recycled construction materials, reforestation and utilizing natural springs for water. Look for the Certification for Sustainable Tourism (CST) logo when choosing accommodations. It acknowledges lodging operators who are minimizing their impact on the environment.

Eat local. Fruit stands, supermarkets and roadside stalls offer an abundance of fresh produce. Try local delicacies like *mamon chino* (rambutan) or *maracuya* (passionfruit), or tropical treats like mango and *sandía* (watermelon). You'll support local farmers and the environment.

BARBARA ASH/SHUTTERSTOCK ©

SUPPORT LOCAL

Book excursions with tour operators who specialize in locally run ecotourism and rural tourism. Use Lokal (lokaltravel.com), Osa Wild (osawild.travel) and Asociación Talamanqueña de Ecoturismo y Conservación (ateccr.org) to ensure your money goes directly to locals without agencies taking a big cut.

Patronize Tico-owned businesses such as *sodas* (small local restaurants) and local artisan markets when eating or buying souvenirs to directly support locals.

CLIMATE CHANGE & TRAVEL

It's impossible to ignore the impact we have when traveling, and the importance of making changes where we can. Lonely Planet urges all travelers to engage with their travel carbon footprint. There are many carbon calculators online that allow travelers to estimate the carbon emissions generated by their journey; try resurgence.org/resources/carbon-calculator.html. Many airlines and booking sites offer travelers the option of offsetting the impact of greenhouse gas emissions by contributing to climate-friendly initiatives around the world. We continue to offset the carbon footprint of all Lonely Planet staff travel, while recognizing this is a mitigation more than a solution.

RESOURCES
turismo-sostenible.co.cr
sinac.go.cr
ateccr.org
terraba.org

UNIQUE AND LOCAL WAYS TO STAY

As an international leader in ecotourism, Costa Rica has a plethora of ecolodges and sustainable lodging options. They range from luxurious high-end hotels to cozy, low-frills family cabins, with options for travelers across the spectrum. The through line is that many travelers want to be surrounded by, and connected to, the country's natural grandeur.

HOW MUCH FOR A

hostel
US$21

hotel
US$125

all-inclusive resort
US$500

HOMESTAYS

Staying with a family is one of the best ways to learn about Costa Rica and its people. Many families in rural and remote areas have cabins on their property that they rent out to visitors. They often include home-cooked meals and specific excursions that reflect the culture and attractions of the area. At El Descanso Terraba, stay within a Brörán community in cabins on their family's ancestral land. In Providencia de Dota, Cabinas Colibri offers a couple of cozy cabins hosted by a local family that also runs nature tours.

SURF CAMPS

Make your surfing dreams come true at a surf camp stay on Península de Nicoya. Numerous camps offer seven- to 10-day programs to teach beginners fundamentals, or to help expert surfers enhance their existing skills. These packages usually include accommodations, equipment, meals, local transportation and daily lessons.

CAMPING

Camp under the stars in a national park. Several parks, including Santa Rosa, Marina Ballena and Palo Verde, have dedicated campgrounds with potable water, outhouses, fire pits and picnic tables. Rent a tent-top 4WD or camper van and stay at secluded beaches near Gandoca National Wildlife Refuge or Playa Zapotal in Guanacaste.

TREEHOUSES & BUNGALOWS

Your inner child will be overjoyed to spend the night in an actual treehouse in the middle of the rainforest. The Maquenque Lodge (Boca Tapada; pictured above) has treehouses 12m above the ground with unobstructed views. No buildings or other treehouses are in sight because it's a 10-minute hike from the main lodge. Rooms have everything you'd need, including hot water, coffee and tea maker, a minibar and a furnished terrace. They also include one screen wall so they're completely open to the sights and sounds of the forest. A full breakfast, a guided hike and canoeing on the nearby lagoon are all included in the price.

For another immersive experience, Tami Lodge is in the mountains of Providencia de Dota between Parque Nacional Los Quetzales and Los Santos Forest Reserve. It offers roomy tented bungalows with private bathrooms and open views of the forest. You can totally disconnect from the outside world because Tami Lodge doesn't have electricity. It uses solar lighting to direct you to the rooms at night and has portable lamps in each tent, so you're not totally in the dark. Don't worry, wi-fi is available in the main lodge, but do yourself a favor and just appreciate the gorgeousness of the surrounding highlands, the coffee plantations and the Río Savegre.

BOOKING

Book your lodging six months in advance for travel during the peak tourist season (December through March) when accommodations fill up quickly. The busiest times, particularly for coastal destinations, are the holiday season around Christmas and New Year, and Semana Santa (Easter Week) because of the influx of international tourists and domestic tourists from San José.

Depending on the type of accommodations, most travelers can book hotels on usual sites:

Booking.com Full spectrum of accommodations from hostels to high-end hotels.

Expedia.com Search for the best deals on hotels, B&Bs and eco-lodges.

TripAdvisor.com Travel review site that also allows users to book lodging.

Airbnb The go-to for home-sharing rentals, especially for solo travelers or families.

VRBO Home-sharing rentals; particularly helpful for large families or groups.

Hostelworld.com Specializes in booking hostel stays but also includes B&Bs.

Booksurfcamps.com Helps you book and compare surf camps.

ALL-INCLUSIVE

All-inclusive options are available for those looking for a contained and easy vacation experience. Most all-inclusive hotels are located in Guanacaste or along the Pacific coast and many are adults-only.

ESSENTIAL NUTS-AND-BOLTS

DRONES

Flying a drone is legal in Costa Rica, but foreign flyers must be registered with the Direccion General de Aviacion Civil (DGAC).

4WD REQUIRED

A 4WD is required to navigate unpaved roads, river crossings and remote regions, especially during rainy season.

PUBLIC BATHROOMS

Especially at beaches, expect to pay a small fee for use and for toilet paper. It's usually 50 to 100 colones, so carry small change with you when heading to the bathroom.

FAST FACTS

Time Zone
CST (-6 GMT)

Country Code
+506

Electricity
110V/60Hz

GOOD TO KNOW

The legal drinking age is 18.

- - - - - - - - - - - - - - - -

Visitors from most countries in Europe, North America and South America are allowed to stay in the country for a maximum of 90 days.

- - - - - - - - - - - - - - - -

Costa Rica has no military.

- - - - - - - - - - - - - - - -

Costa Rica uses the metric system.

- - - - - - - - - - - - - - - -

The national language is Spanish, but in tourist destinations most people also speak English.

ACCESSIBLE TRAVEL

Under Costa Rican law it's mandatory for all public and private establishments to provide accessible services. Check out the Costa Rica Accessible Tourism Network (costaricaturismoaccesible.com).

Many national parks have accessible trails for people with limited mobility. Check in advance at the SINAC (Sistema Nacional de Áreas de Conservación; sinac.go.cr).

Red Costaricense de Turismo Acesible (Costa Rican Network of Accessible Tourism; costaricaturismoaccesible.com/donatapa/playa-accesible) has created wheelchair-accessible paths and entrances for certain beaches across Costa Rica.

Hotels are more likely to be wheelchair accessible than rental homes.

Many tour companies and bloggers offer packages for wheelchair users, and people who have hearing or vision impairments. Check out the following websites: ilviaggiocr.com/accessiblecr, curbfreewithcorylee.com and deafresorts.com.

FAMILY TRAVEL

Rental homes are the best way to accommodate large families, especially multigenerational. Some families enjoy all-inclusive resorts because all restaurants and activities are in one place and already paid for.

If traveling with a large group, consider hiring your own driver. Driving a large expensive vehicle like a minivan around unfamiliar and possibly dangerous roads with your family aboard is stressful. So let an expert handle it!

Booking private tours ensures the guide is focused on your family.

Many nature and adventure activities and tours are geared for families, especially children. Tour operators often offer excursions like ziplining, horseback riding, sloth encounters and water sports that are designed for travelers of all ages.

BEST IN TRAVEL

Lonely Planet honored Costa Rica with a 2021 'Best in Travel' award for its commitment to accessible tourism.

TRAVEL INSURANCE

Always get travel insurance in case of any inclement weather or natural disasters, injuries during activities, illnesses or other unexpected emergencies.

PUBLIC HOLIDAYS

Semana Santa (Easter Week) is a major holiday. Domestic travel spikes and many businesses close throughout the week.

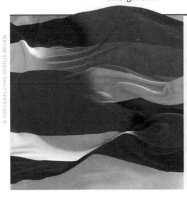

LGBTIQ+ TRAVELERS

Costa Rica is one of the most liberal countries in the region for LGBTIQ+ rights, legalizing gay marriage, allowing transgender people to change their gender on legal documents, and passing antidiscrimination laws codifying penalties for hate crimes.

A Roman Catholic country, it's still relatively socially conservative, so there may be cultural stigma in more rural locations.

San José and Manuel Antonio host annual Pride events, and have LGBTIQ+ hotels, bars and clubs.

Puerto Viejo on the Caribbean coast and Santa Teresa in the Península de Nicoya are also welcoming to queer travelers.

LANGUAGE

Spanish pronunciation is easy, as most sounds have equivalents in English. Also, Spanish spelling is phonetically consistent, meaning that there's a clear and consistent relationship between what you see in writing and how it's pronounced.

If you read our pronunciation guides as if they were English, you'll be understood. Note that *kh* is a throaty sound (like the '*ch*' in the Scottish loch), v and b are like a soft English '*v*' (between a '*v*' and a '*b*'), and *r* is strongly rolled. The stressed syllables are in italics in our pronunciation guides.

BASICS

Hello.	*Hola.*	o·la
Goodbye.	*Adiós.*	a·dyos
Yes.	*Sí.*	see
No.	*No.*	no
Please.	*Por favor.*	por fa·vor
Thank you.	*Gracias.*	gra·syas
Excuse me.	*Con permiso.*	kon per·mee·so
Sorry.	*Perdón.*	per·don

What's your name?
¿Cómo se   ko·mo se
llama usted?   ya·ma oo·sted (polite)
¿Cómo te llamas?   ko·mo te ya·mas (informal)

My name is ...
Me llamo ...   me ya·mo ...

Do you speak English?
¿Habla inglés?   a·bla een·gles (polite)
¿Hablas inglés?   a·blas een·gles (informal)

I don't understand.
Yo no entiendo.   yo no en·tyen·do

TIME & NUMBERS

What time is it?	*¿Qué hora es?*	ke o·ra es
It's (10) o'clock.	*Son (las diez).*	son (las dyes)
Half past (1).	*Es (la una) y media.*	es (la oo·na) ee me·dya
morning	*mañana*	ma·nya·na
afternoon	*tarde*	tar·de
evening	*noche*	no·che
yesterday	*ayer*	a·yer
today	*hoy*	oy
tomorrow	*mañana*	ma·nya·na

1	*uno*	oo·no		**6**	*seis*	seys
2	*dos*	dos		**7**	*siete*	sye·te
3	*tres*	tres		**8**	*ocho*	o·cho
4	*cuatro*	kwa·tro		**9**	*nueve*	nwe·ve
5	*cinco*	seen·ko		**10**	*diez*	dyes

EMERGENCIES

Help!	*¡Socorro!*	so·ko·ro
Go away!	*¡Váyase!*	va·ya·se
Call a ...!	*¡Llame a ...!*	ya·me a...
the police	*la policía*	la po·lee·see·a
a doctor	*un doctor*	oon dok·tor
I'm lost.	*Estoy perdido/a.*	es·toy per·dee·do/a (m/f)

Index

000 Map pages

000 Map pages

000 Map pages

258

'I had to hold back tears when I saw a mama whale and her baby on the boat ride to Parque Nacional Corcovado (p224). It was so beautiful!'

JANNA ZINZI

'On my birthday, I woke up to a rare clear view of Volcán Arenal (pictured left; p118). Mother Nature's birthday present.'

MARA VORHEES

'Volcán Irazú (p68) holds a special place in my heart and each visit feels unique. It's always an adventure and the view feels, in every way, transcendent.'

ROBERT ISENBERG

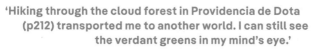

'Hiking through the cloud forest in Providencia de Dota (p212) transported me to another world. I can still see the verdant greens in my mind's eye.'

JANNA ZINZI

'That time I got some uninvited guests at my jungle treehouse – a band of coatis (pictured right) escaping the rain.'

MARA VORHEES

TOP MARCEL QUESADA/SHUTTERSTOCK ©
BOTTOM BUCHPITZER/SHUTTERSTOCK ©

THIS BOOK

Design development
Lauren Egan, Tina García, Fergal Condon

Content development
Anne Mason

Cartography development
Wayne Murphy, Katerina Pavkova

Production development
Mario D'Arco, Dan Moore, Sandie Kestell, Virginia Moreno, Juan Winata

Series development leadership
Liz Heynes, Darren O'Connell, Piers Pickard, Chris Zeiher

Destination editor
Amy Lynch

Production editor
Amy Lysen

Cartographer
Alison Lyall

Book designer
Virginia Moreno

Assisting editors
Fionnuala Twomey, Simon Williamson

Cover researcher
Norma Brewer

Thanks James Appleton, Gwen Cotter, Joel Cotterell, Clare Healy, Victoria Harrison, John Taufa